CHOOSE YOUR OWN APOCALYPSE

WITH KIM JONG-UN & FRIENDS

Also by Rob Sears

The Beautiful Poetry of Donald Trump
Vladimir Putin: Life Coach

Acknowledgements

Much gratitude to Hannah Knowles, Jamie Byng and Gordon Wise for helping me choose the right adventure, to Leila Cruickshank, Vicki Rutherford, Aa'Ishah Hawton and Lucy Zhou for heroic work against a ticking clock, and to the 3M corporation for inventing Post-it Notes. Special thanks also to Grace for always looking me in the eye and dropping her next move, and to both our families for being supportive beyond any call of duty.

CHOOSE YOUR OWN APOCALYPSE

WITH KIM JONG-UN & FRIENDS

Rob Sears

CANONGATE

First published in Great Britain, the USA and Canada in 2019
by Canongate Books Ltd, 14 High Street, Edinburgh EH1 1TE

Distributed in the USA by Publishers Group West and in Canada by
Publishers Group Canada

canongate.co.uk

2

British Library Cataloguing-in-Publication Data
A catalogue record for this book is available on
request from the British Library

ISBN 978 1 78689 864 7

Typeset in Archer by Palimpsest Book Production Ltd,
Falkirk, Stirlingshire

Printed and bound in Great Britain by Clays Ltd, Elcograf S.p.A.

NOW RECRUITING

Can YOU keep a calm head in emergencies? Do YOU know how to 'manage upwards' while maintaining a client-centric attitude? And are YOU ready to make the choices that will determine the future of human civilisation?

Then there may be an entry-level position waiting for you at the United Nations' Department for Continuity (Global).

Send your CV to Susan at
UNContinuityDept@gmail.com

It's been six months since you answered an ad and began your job as a junior officer at the UN Department for Continuity (Global).

Based in a former toiletries supply room on the third floor of UN headquarters, your team's job is to 'prevent the untimely cessation of global activities in any given year', or, in layman's terms, to stop the world ending.

Basically, you are the ones world leaders call when the proverbial shitstorm is about to hit the proverbial windfarm.

But none of that matters right now because it's five p.m. on Christmas Eve and you're heading home for the holidays. Your computer is shutting down and you're just putting your coat on when your boss saunters over with a greasy grin on his face.

'We've just had a Code Red from Pink Camellia.' You recognise the codename for North Korea's Kim Jong-un. 'Something about a missing rocket, I think he said. Would you be a star and pop over to Pyongyang to make sure everything's OK? I'd go myself but I'm on Christmas dinner duties tomorrow. I'm doing a bird within a bird within a bird, have you ever tried it?'

Typical. Quiet all month then this. What do you want to do?

→ **Tell him where he can stuff his three-bird roast. You're not cancelling your Christmas plans for anything. Turn to page 27.**

→ **Spring into action. A nuclear conflagration would spoil the holiday season for everyone. Turn to page 113.**

Abandoning your car, you approach the sinkhole cautiously. Its sides are dauntingly steep, but you want to see what's going on in there first-hand, so you begin to clamber down the rock walls. As carefully as you choose your hand and footholds, the freshly settled earth is loose and you find yourself slip-sliding down the last few metres, landing painfully atop the pile of wrecked SUVs.

It's dark down here. You dust yourself off and switch on your phone's torch.

You're in a perfectly circular tunnel, easily twice your height, stretching off into darkness. The walls are smooth and warm as if freshly dug, and from the darkness ahead, a low whirring sound reaches you. You advance forwards, running the light beam along the walls and ceilings and wishing you had a weapon.

You haven't walked more than ten or fifteen metres before your torchlight picks out what appears to be a gigantic steel drill-bit. Completely filling the circumference of the tunnel ahead, it must be one of Blue Poppy's inventions – maybe some kind of tunnelling machine.

Almost silently, it rotates towards you, causing a glowing red light attached to it to describe circles in the gloom. You gulp.

Somehow you feel as if this colossal machine is watching you.

'Hello?' you say, feeling foolish for trying to communicate with what is probably a bit of inanimate mining equipment.

A small hatch in the thing opens and a flimsy plastic extendable arm pops out.

It would almost be comical if it were not carrying a pistol that's pointing straight at your head.

→ **Retreat back up the tunnel immediately. You have no idea what you're dealing with. Turn to page 107.**

→ **Whatever this thing is, you don't like it one bit. Fight it mano-a-machine. Turn to page 47.**

At first Kim Jong-un murmurs nonsensical sounds, but like an old radio tuning in he begins recounting his past to the hushed room.

Kim Jong-un remembers being the only kid with a bodyguard at his Swiss school.

He remembers trying to start an epic prank war with his best friend, who didn't dare prank him back.

He remembers the day his dad named him Great Successor but being more excited about watching *Space Jam*.

'Think further forward in time,' you prompt. 'Three years ago, do you remember a code?'

He goes quiet for a while, then resumes.

He remembers his first taste of brie.

He remembers his trousers getting too tight around his middle, and one day finding they'd all been swapped for a larger size.

He remembers the shock of surfing Netflix one night on the nation's only account and stumbling on his dad as a puppet in the movie *Team America*. Pretty funny, he thought.

The hypnotherapist interrupts to tell you that Kim Jong-un should be woken.

'Being under this long could be very dangerous,' she urges.

→ **Snap him out of it. Turn to page 96.**

→ **He still hasn't remembered any kind of code. You have to keep going. Turn to page 9.**

'I want to save the bees as much as you do,' you say, advancing with extreme caution towards the demented lab director. Perhaps if you can get close enough, you can seize her handheld detonator. 'But blowing us both up won't help the bees. Now why don't you deactivate the bomb and unlock the door, and we can both go outside and save the bees together?'

'Don't come any closer!' she hisses, brandishing the device in front of her like a protective wand . . . but as you get closer, you realise you have seen one like it before. On your keyring.

Suddenly you laugh.

'Are you going to shine your pocket torch at me?' You stride over to the 'bomb' and unravel some masking tape and loo rolls. 'Are you going to blow us up with these toilet rolls?'

She shrugs her shoulders and turns away. 'You got me. But I'm not sorry. It was the only way to get you to listen.'

It's a sad scene. She's used and abused your goodwill and given you quite a fright – but at the same time you can't help but think how desperate she must be to go to such lengths. If she really believes the world faces an existential threat, can you fault her for going to extremes?

What do you want to do?

→ **Help her save the bees after all. Turn to page 56.**

→ **Get out of here and find a proper apocalypse. Turn to page 116.**

You're being taxied to the runway in an Aeroflot jumbo jet when it all goes to pieces. Perhaps thirty seconds earlier and you'd have made it safely into the sky.

From your seat you cannot see what has caused the plane to stop. Then the brainless horde sways into view and begins scaling the aircraft. You have never seen anything like it. There are hundreds of them, passengers and airport staff alike, swarming up the wheel arches and onto the wings, pulling everything apart with the strength of fanatics. An airport policewoman is popping rivets off the plane with her fingernails.

The pilot tells everyone not to panic but it's far too late for that, because they've pulled off the door, and now steel is being divided into scraps, engines into components, and bodies into bits of flesh, just as elsewhere unions are being divided into members, countries into regions, villages into squabbling families and debating positions into polar extremes, such is the power of this dread meme. It's as though time-lapse maggots are eating the human world, and that's not the sort of thing that goes down well back at the office.

Whoopsie. Perhaps you should have gone to page 105 and headed for the motorway instead.

The End

You run to the side door in time to see the Falcon 9 spacecraft thundering slowly into the sky. In its windows you can see Elon Musk and all six Uncanny Elons waving goodbye. Evidently they don't fancy their chances against the new virtual overlords of Earth and are going to try life on Mars instead.

This isn't looking good.

→ **Continue to page 69.**

Maybe it's a contrarian impulse but something makes you think you should deal with China first. Your boss gave you the authority to decide and, high off your hat-trick, you choose to go with your gut. You just hope they've got a proper, meaty global disaster for you so you don't have to tell him you made the wrong call.

You sleep for virtually the entire journey, just peeling your eyes open long enough to shuffle through airport security and into the car that's been sent to pick you up from Beijing Airport. When you wake again, the car has stopped, the sun is high in the sky and an energetic Chinese woman in a white coat is shaking you awake and introducing herself as Professor Wu, director of the Ecology Maintenance Institute.

'They finally sent someone,' she says. 'You wouldn't believe how many messages I sent. Follow me and I'll show you the lab.'

With a disconcertingly strong grip on your arm, she steers you to a nondescript plaster building with flowers growing on the roof. You blink groggily and allow yourself to be led.

The feel-good effect of the meme seems to have abandoned you as quickly as it came, making way for a pounding headache.

→ **Follow Prof. Wu inside. Turn to page 100.**

'Keep remembering,' you say softly. From his rapid eye movement, you can see Kim Jong-un is drifting deeper into his trance . . . perhaps dangerously deep.

Kim Jong-un remembers the twinkly eyes of his uncle Jang Song-thaek, just after having had the head removed from his corpse.

He remembers bored afternoons bouncing his dad's Michael Jordan-signed basketball around the Palace of the Sun.

Above all, he says, he remembers what Denmark did – and suddenly he's leapt out of his chair and is running around like a cannonball, shouting incoherently about Danish fiends and revenge.

The hypnotherapist snaps her fingers and Kim Jong-un comes around immediately.

'I remember the code,' he says triumphantly. 'We can deactivate the rocket. But first,' he points a sweeping arm at you, '*you* are an agent of the Vikings. Seize the invader!'

The bodyguards look at each other and at the generals, as confused as you are, but they aren't about to disobey. They grab you by the arms and heave you off, struggling.

→ **What the heck is going on? Turn to page 22.**

You need the fastest way out of the city available so you follow the signs for Brussels Airport, twice swerving to avoid the mad shufflers. As you get out of town you see fewer of the meme zombies but you don't slow down until you reach airport drop-offs, where you abandon the car and run into the airport. It's crowded with people, but everyone here seems reassuringly normal.

'How can I help you?' smiles the man at the ticket desk.

Phew, it looks like you're going to be OK.

→ **Continue to page 6.**

Inside the bistro a dozen or so well-coiffed bureaucrats are being waited on with trays of oysters, but despite the opulence of the surroundings the mood is anxious.

'We've set this up as our temporary operations centre,' your client tells you. 'Something very strange is happening on our continent.'

You mention your sighting of Angela Merkel and she nods as you take seats in a corner booth.

'So it's got Merkel, too? More and more people are losing their minds. Ever since Christmas Day, we've had reports of fistfights in national parliaments, sports teams disbanding, old allies turning on each other. It's as if people are losing all ability to get on with one another.'

'What could be causing it?'

'At first it was a total mystery. But we believe we have identified the cause.'

She slides an attaché case onto the table between you.

→ **Attack the case. Whatever this thing is, it needs to be destroyed. Turn to page 16.**

→ **Ask what's inside. Turn to page 70.**

Trump's reassuring words to the nation are slightly undermined by the fact that he is dressed in a full hazmat suit

It's midday on New Year's Eve by the time you finally arrive at the White House. An ashen-faced page shows you through to a crowded Oval Office and you join the hushed gathering at the rear, though not before grabbing one of the room-temperature Big Macs stacked on a seventeenth-century side table.

The crowd watches solemnly as President Donald Trump addresses a TV camera from behind his great desk.

'Folks, I know you've seen the reports on CNN. They're saying there's a mystery disease called Virus X. They're saying it's killed half the people in Washington already and it's spreading fast. That my whole cabinet is dead. That Donald J. Trump has only survived because of my germophobia. Don't believe it, folks. I hate to use this word, but Virus X is bullcrap. Total bullcrap. They just make this stuff up because their ratings are a disaster. I'm telling you, I'm here in DC and everything is completely normal.'

The president's reassuring words are slightly undermined by the fact that he is dressed in full hazmat, as are several of the officials in the crowd, while others wear facemasks. You're about to ask the man next to you if there are any spares lying around, when you notice he is sobbing softly into his shirt collar.

→ **Quietly ask the man if he's OK. Turn to page 122.**

→ **Keep listening to Trump. Turn to page 33.**

'Are you calling Elon Musk?' Prof. Wu asks apprehensively.

'If anyone can help, it's him.'

'We can't rely on him to solve every problem!'

This is a bit rich after you've agreed to help her. 'I've figured out the solution already – robot bees – we just need my good friend Elon to start a company to build them.'

Your call goes to answerphone, so you hang up and try dialling again.

'I also think the idea of building robot bees is highly arrogant,' Prof. Wu continues. 'The bee has been precision-honed to pollinate over millions of years of evolution.'

'Evolution didn't do that great a job, though, or they wouldn't all be dying. Also robot bees could be way better. They could turn into little submarines so they don't die when they fall into a glass of lemonade. And have tasers instead of stings.'

The call goes to answerphone again. It seems Elon Musk's gratitude for helping to stop his Really Freakishly Large Drill doesn't extend to answering your calls.

What do you want to try instead?

→ **Take a look at the bees in the lab. Turn to page 52.**

→ **Try to get hold of President Xi. Turn to page 150.**

A couple of flights and a long layover later, you're approaching the source of Blue Poppy's distress call: a huge desert ranch in Nevada. Your company expense account will only stretch to a hire car in the Super Economy category, and the crappy suspension makes for a bone-shaking ride up the unpaved approach road.

As you get near you see an aircraft hangar-style structure with SUVs parked outside with various company logos: SpaceX, Tesla, The Boring Company, OpenAI. Then there is a KAAWUMPH and all the vehicles are gone, replaced by a billowing cloud of sand.

Whoa! A sinkhole the size of a tennis court has swallowed them up.

As a subterranean thrum passes under you, you stop the car and jump out, wondering what under the earth you are letting yourself in for.

→ **Run to the hangar-like building. Turn to page 38.**

→ **Climb into the sinkhole. Turn to page 2.**

In a sudden motion you reach across and grab the attaché case, scrabbling at the security clasp. When it doesn't open you fling the case at the wall, bashing it repeatedly against the doorway to the bathrooms.

On looking up from your exertions you find the bureaucrats staring at you.

'Don't you want to know what's inside first?' your client asks.

That'd be wise, you must concede.

→ **Ask what's in the case. Turn to page 70.**

You sit cross-legged on your bamboo mat, watching the zero-carbon farming blimps glide among the green pepperpot hills of Guangxi. The year is 2050. Your life only really began, as you see it now, following your encounter with the director of the bee institute. Since then you've worked tirelessly to preserve the world's insect habitats, bicycling from village to village spreading word of sustainable agricultural practices.

Through the dedication of many people such as yourself, and the new global environmental laws eventually secured by Prof. Wu, the world is now on a better track. Not that you take any credit. You're just proud to have been part of a truly collective global effort.

Since you found your new calling you haven't been in touch with your boss. You did hear of a disease emanating from Washington DC that made you think of your old life. It wiped out over a billion people all told – to your current way of thinking a needed cull of an unsupportable global population.

A dozen wire-tailed swallows swoop low past where you're sitting, chasing the plentiful bugs.

Something makes you look up.

→ **If you're feeling lucky turn to page 117.**

→ **If you've used up all your luck (be honest!), turn to page 121.**

'We can't stop the rocket, but we've got to warn the Americans,' you tell Kim Jong-un and his advisors. 'We've still got three hours until impact. Who knows how many lives they can save if they evacuate now?'

Some of the generals confer. 'Marshal Chairman, we think the foreigner's advice is wise. If we warn the Americans, they'll know it was an accident. It could stop them retaliating.'

Kim Jong-un signals his assent, and the officials get busy setting up an urgent diplomatic phone call. The oldest general is given the honour of being spokesman for North Korea.

'Hello, Mr Vice President,' he says warmly. 'How is your family?' He continues with further pleasantries for, you feel, a little too long. 'The reason I'm calling? Well, it's a little embarrassing, but later on today New York City is going to be hit by one of our old missiles that was inadvertently not destroyed, but I want you to know it's a complete accident . . . Three hours . . . That's true, three hours isn't very long . . . Yes, I agree, we'll try and give you more notice next time . . . No, I hope there won't be a next time either, Mr Vice President . . . I agree, you can't evacuate a whole city in three hours, but if we can together save even a few lives, I think you'll agree it's worth a try, don't you?'

'Tell him to save the New York Knicks,' Kim Jong-un chips in. 'Patrick Ewing, Kevin Knox.'

'I can tell you're upset. But the fact is, it was an accident . . . Yes, that's true, we have made threats in the past ... That was just sabre-rattling, we would never harm any of your citizens ... That's true, some of your hostages have been harmed, good point ... But, Mike, I hope you agree, it wouldn't be sporting to retaliate for an innocent mistake? ... All right, Mike, you go and do your thing if you have to. Always good speaking with you.'

The oldest general slowly replaces the receiver on the conference phone.

'He was really nice about it. But he said he's got no choice. He's launched a pre-emptive strike. We've got seven minutes.'

Everyone looks at the clock.

'Has anyone got any jokes?' Kim Jong-un enquires. No one speaks, so he cracks: 'If we survive this I'm going to have you all executed.'

Nothing left to do now but wait to die, right at the bottom of the career ladder.

The End

It's 2035.

Everyone is in high spirits as the boiled potato is brought to the table and sliced into twenty.

'To our first Martian-grown vegetable!' says Bill Gates, and the other billionaires all raise imaginary glasses while sipping electrolytes from their hydration packs.

You were lucky to reach Nevada on the Harley just as Elon Musk was putting the finishing touches to his prototype Mars lander. He'd not been planning to set off to the Red Planet until a whole battery of tests was complete, but when you told him how hopeless the Virus X situation was, he decided to throw caution to the wind and take you with him.

At first it was just you, Musk and his on-again, off-again girlfriend, Grimes, and you always felt like a third wheel. Then billionaires Jeff and MacKenzie Bezos arrived by coincidence on the same day in separate spacecraft, adding a whole new dimension of awkwardness. But by and by others followed and, when Richard Branson stepped out of his Virgin-branded landing pod, the party really began to heat up.

These days, the 3D-printed dome structures you all live in have become home to quite a community.

The news you've been getting from Earth is pretty gloomy; while the death toll from Virus X was only a billion, insect decline and climate change have ravaged the planet. But you try not to think too much about that now. You've got enough responsibility here running the Mars Continuity Team, a special unit charged with preventing your pioneer civilisation from being wiped out by dust storms, super-volcanoes or space radiation.

OK, you didn't stop the apocalypse, but your work continues.

The End

Kim Jong-un's guard drags you to a damp, windowless cell elsewhere in the palace and locks the door.

'I'm not Danish!' you call through the bars. 'I haven't even been to Denmark as the frequency of apocalyptic incidents in that nation is too low to warrant it!'

You sit down on the hard floor, unsure how to feel. On one hand, Kim Jong-un said he remembered the code, so your assignment has, you hope, been a success. On the other, you have no idea what he has against Denmark all of a sudden, and you've definitely read stories about North Korean prisoners being thrown to packs of hungry dogs, something you'd ideally like to avoid.

Hours pass.

Then days.

Now and then you hear far-off gunfire and shouting. Sometimes the floor shakes. After one such episode, a pipe in the ceiling begins leaking a steady film of water down the wall that you're able to lick, but how long can a person survive without food?

One day, you see a rat sitting in the near darkness of the cell's corner. It must have come in through the ceiling.

'It's me, Dennis Rodman,' the rat says, without moving its lips. 'I know a way out.'

→ **Follow the rat. Turn to page 25.**

→ **Eat it instead. Turn to page 80.**

Regular psychoanalysis, in your view, is the only way to help Svetlana dig deep and rediscover her inner idealist, so that for the first time in her life she'll be able to create a meme that brings people back together and thus dezombify the citizens of Europe.

'Therapy? Sure, I'll give it a go. Maybe I'll remember something really bad that happened to me, other than being born,' she says hopefully.

Although you have no training in this area, you fancy yourself as a natural. After all, making your clients feel listened to is 90 per cent of this job. You drag a couch over from a soft breakout area and begin the work. Nihilistic though Svetlana may be, like most people she likes to talk about herself, and it's gratifyingly easy to get her started.

She tells you about her childhood in Kaliningrad. From a young age she was a skilled influencer, engineering her parents' divorce so she could get two sets of pocket money. Her favourite game was institutionalising headmistresses at the various schools she worked her way through.

As she tells you about her early life, the TV in the corner livestreams the RT news network. From the muted images being broadcast, you can see the fabric of Europe quickly unravelling, subhuman crowds mustering superhuman strength to pull the Eiffel Tower down and surging into the Reichstag.

It can't be long before Moscow too is engulfed – but there's no rushing the work of the analyst.

→ **Keep going patiently. Turn to page 86.**

The chopper pilot decreases altitude and swivels so he can land on the highway on the far side of the barricade, pointing back towards the infected lobbyists. They scatter, running over the central reservation and into the wasteland on either side of the empty highway.

You grab a stun gun from the chopper and leap onto the asphalt, unleashing a precision salvo of anaesthetic darts. THWUK, THWUK, THWUK. The lobbyists keep stumbling along, making desperate final farewell calls to their corporate clients, but they'll soon pass out.

You're hauling the nearest lobbyist's limp body back to the chopper when you see another lobbyist running low through the gap in the barbed wire, then another. You drop the body and take down a couple of the infected, but it's hopeless. There are too many of them, and you're out of sleeper darts.

If it wasn't already, Virus X is now well and truly loose.

'Told you,' says the chief epidemiologist, who hasn't moved from his seat in the chopper.

With the city blockade breached and your hopes of containing the outbreak dashed, the only thing left is to return to the White House. But when the pilot tries to restart the engine, it stutters and fails.

'What the — the tank's empty! Someone must have cut the fuel line!'

You've no choice but to begin the three-mile trek back to Pennsylvania Avenue on foot.

→ **Continue to page 141.**

You blink at the rat Dennis Rodman.

'You look different,' you tell him. There seems to be a long delay between thinking something and saying it. 'Did Kim Jong-un do this to you?'

'I know a way out,' the famous basketball-playing rodent repeats. 'Follow me.'

Dennis Rodman slowly levitates and melts through the ceiling like a ghost.

It occurs to you that you are probably hallucinating due to lack of food and resultant organ failure.

You wonder if you would have ended up here if you'd cut off the hypnotherapy session earlier (if only you could go back to page 4 and find out).

Little feet scamper over your legs but you're too weak even to move.

Farewell, Dennis Rodman. Farewell, beautiful career.

The End

What just happened? Sadly you'll never know, because you and everyone else you know have just been vaporised

There's no way you're going to be the sucker who spends Christmas working while your boss indulges his culinary fancies in his no doubt obscenely large kitchen.

'Deal with it yourself,' you tell the old scrooge, and head for the exit. He calls after you – his usual guilt-trip shtick about the fate of humanity – but you're not falling for it this time. Besides, whatever the crisis, you'll be able to deal with it better when you come back rested and clear-headed in the new year.

But a couple of days later, you are happily ensconced in your armchair, digesting a leftover turkey sandwich and watching a Hollywood disaster movie, when all the windows smash, a scalding wind rushes in and everything goes black.

What just happened?

Sadly you'll never know, because you, your festively sweatered family and everyone else have been vaporised into your constituent atoms.

It was a quick, reasonably painless way to go, but disappointingly anticlimactic compared to the movie you were watching, and not even as narratively satisfying.

The End

You tell your minder you're going to the bathroom, then climb out of the window and make a dash for the west gate. Kim Jong-un's sister is waiting in the shadows, her collar turned up.

'Follow me.'

A few minutes later, the pair of you are sitting in a North Korean version of Starbucks, drinking caramel macchiatos through straws beneath a painting of the Brilliant Comrade that dispenses napkins through the O of his mouth.

'A lot has changed here since 2017,' she tells you. 'Back then, all my little brother and the gang thought about were rockets. They launched twenty in one year, every one going higher and further! We got to 3,000km above sea level, no lie. People were taking us seriously at last. We were on CNN.' She smiles wistfully. 'Then we tried to blow the moon out of the sky.'

'You did what?'

'The Americans landed on the moon. My brother wanted us to go one better and smash it to bits! But we lost our rocket. For eighteen months we thought it had been a dud. Then last week, we re-established contact.' Her voice wavers. 'We never meant to hurt anyone, just explode the stupid moon and mess around with the tides a little. I guess our eyes were too big for our bellies!'

You offer her a napkin to blot her tears. 'There, there, I'm sure anyone hellbent on terrifying the world into letting them continue brainwashing their people would have done the same.'

'If only he could remember the recall code!' she blubs.

'There's a recall code?'

'Don't tell him I told you!' Kim Sol-song pleads. 'Being his sister doesn't protect me. You know what he did to our uncle.'

The uncle, isn't he the one who got poisoned at the airport? Or the one who was killed by firing squad? Your knowledge of the family's history is sketchy. Regardless, you've got to retrieve that code.

→ **Continue to page 142.**

She smacks her head. 'Of course! I myself helped draft the primary legislation for the EU Emergency Broadcast Protocol. It never occurred to me we might actually use it! I've got the software right here on my laptop.'

She clicks and taps with one finger.

'With this system I can send an SMS message to reach over 80 per cent of EU citizens within an hour. There!'

She taps her enter key with a flourish and lo and behold, your phone instantly buzzes.

You read your new message:

FOR YOUR OWN SAFETY AND THAT OF
THOSE AROUND YOU, DO NOT CHECK
YOUR SOCIAL MEDIA

Your heart sinks even as your thumb resists the magnetic pull of the Facebook icon. The high-ranking functionary seems to have made a basic error in human psychology.

'That should stop it spreading any further,' she says brightly, upon which, on cue, half a dozen bricks fly through the upper, unboarded part of the windows facing the street, smashing wine glasses and smacking one official in the back of the head, causing him to go rather brutally facedown into a freshly risen cheese soufflé. You peer through a gap in the boards to see a group of freshly radicalised federal police running off down the avenue.

'There goes our security detail,' someone says.

Trying to stop the meme spreading has backfired. You're going to need a different approach.

'Can't we do an electromagnetic pulse and wipe everyone's phones at once?' your client suggests.

→ **Try to create a countermeme instead. Turn to page 82.**

'I'm going out to the corridor to make a call,' you tell the North Koreans. The situation is worse than you'd feared and frankly above your pay grade.

Your North Korean minder watches as you try to call your boss (he usually knows what to do in tricky workplace circumstances, slimy as he is), but he's not picking up. You try your contact at the Pentagon instead, thinking she may have access to some kind of secret space laser that could shoot down the runaway rocket. But it's Christmas Day and she's not answering either.

As you scroll through your contacts, wondering who else could help, the only woman among the officials, Lieutenant Colonel Kim Sol-song, emerges from the Ops room and sidles over. She's brought the tray of yellow cookies with her.

'Excuse my brother's manners, we forgot to offer you a snack,' she says loudly, and then in a whisper so your minder doesn't hear, adds: 'Let us talk in private. Meet me at the west gate.'

Kim Jong-un's sister? Curious. You thank her and take a chewy yellow disc. It sticks to your tongue.

→ **Sneak out and meet Kim Jong-un's sister at the west gate. Turn to page 28.**

→ **You don't have time for this cloak-and-dagger stuff. Go back to Kim Jong-un and offer to shoot the thing down yourself. Turn to page 102.**

'Maybe you've seen the videos,' Trump continues to the TV camera. 'Lines of bodybags. Exploding pustules. Gushing, purple fluids draining out of every orifice until all that's left is human jerky.' Trump shakes his head scornfully and taps his temple. 'It's not real, people! It's deep-fake footage. They want you to believe I can't protect you. They think you're too stupid to see that since I drained the swamp, this great country has never been so clean and disease-free. So true. Well, I think you people are a lot smarter than that or you wouldn't have given me the greatest victory in history over Crooked Hillary in 2016. The whole map was red. So beautiful. Beautiful victory . . .'

As the president continues to reminisce, you notice the sobbing of the man to your left is growing louder.

→ **Reassure him that it's going to be OK. Turn to page 122.**

You take a scalpel from a medical chest, open the tent flap and advance on the ill-starred fowl. Drumstick's trusting black eyes, framing that brilliant red snood, blink up at you.

About an hour later, you're covered in gizzards, blood and feathers, as well as a few scratches, but you're none the wiser about the cause of the virus. The frank and honest truth is that you have no idea how to dissect a turkey, still less analyse the pathology of a disease, perhaps something you should have reflected on about an hour ago.

Tears are streaming down the chief epidemiologist's face.

'We'll all see you very soon at the big ranch in the sky, big guy. Drumstick,' he mumbles by way of eulogy, 'was the best turkey I ever knew. But a lousy intern.'

You begin hosing the blood off your hazmat suit, keen to feel clean again. The sick thought occurs to you that this is the closest you'll get to Christmas dinner this year, or maybe ever again.

As your thoughts follow this pessimistic turn, you notice Donald Junior sidling across the White House lawn, eyeing you through his visor.

'Making any progress?' he enquires, like he's the boss of you.

There's nothing worse than dealing with clients' children, but this time you don't have to because the chief epidemiologist answers for you.

'No,' he says bluntly. 'It's displacement activity because we can't accept we're all going to die.'

'Excellent!' says Donald Junior, carrying on his way with a skip in his step.

Now what?

→ **Turn to page 78 to try another course of action.**

Somewhere in Kim Jong-un's oversized head is the code that will save the world, or so you hope.

'I'd like to try something called regression hypnosis,' you tell him.

He nods meekly. Acknowledging his fallibility seems to have really knocked the stuffing out of him.

A party of officials is sent out to drum up someone in the city with an NVQ in hypnotherapy. A few hours later, they come back with a very nervous woman in her pyjamas who visibly whitens when she sees the Chairman, as though in the presence of a demigod.

'Don't pussyfoot around, hypnotise me,' Kim Jong-un orders her.

Her hands tremble on the special pendulum she waves in front of him, but soon he does indeed appear to enter a trance-like state.

→ **In a low, relaxing voice, tell Kim Jong-un to start remembering the past. Turn to page 4.**

There are papers, petri dishes and unfinished experiments all over the work benches. Could they contain the secret to producing a vaccination against Virus X? Is that why the scientists were killed? Because they were getting too close to saving humankind?

You try to read a few pages of the deceased researchers' notes, but they're in technical shorthand you can make no sense of. Perhaps for fear of losing their jobs, they wanted to conceal what they were doing. If you want to make sense of them, you're going to need some expert assistance.

Fumbling with your thick rubber gloves on the lab phone keypad, you manage to dial your boss again and a man called Barry you met at a party once. He was some kind of scientist, you're pretty sure. You even try dialling 911, but no one's picking up.

That leaves one person.

Susan.

Pandemics are one of her areas of expertise. She wrote a column about them in *Modern Apocalypse*, your industry magazine, for heaven's sake. Is it time to swallow your pride and do the unthinkable?

→ **Call Susan for help. Turn to page 40.**

→ **No way, you'd rather accept the painful deaths of millions. Try something else instead. Turn back to page 78.**

You step into the vast hangar. At the far end, panoramic windows overlook the pockmarked desert. Near them, a lone figure swipes and taps in mid-air at some kind of nifty holographic display. How the other half work, you think.

'Did someone call about an impending apocalypse?' you say, your voice echoing under the cathedral-high ceiling.

The man does not look up so you walk over. Even as you approach, through the glass further off in the desert you see dust rise up as another huge sinkhole opens.

'Mr Musk, sir? . . . I noticed the ground's a bit unstable outside.'

'I'm busy,' says Elon Musk eventually, manipulating indecipherable code in thin air.

'Can you tell me what's going on?' you say hesitantly. 'I can't help with your catastrophe if I don't know what it is.'

'I didn't ask for help.'

'Oh. Then do you know who called for me?'

Elon Musk is so absorbed in his work you don't think he's heard you, but then he turns and speaks in his clipped South African accent: 'I didn't call anyone. Now leave me alone; you're lowering my IQ just by being here.'

Musk resumes swiping around on his holographic display, then seeing you are still hovering adds: 'Or talk to my friend if you must.'

You're startled to see that standing slightly too close to you is another Elon Musk, this one about 20 per cent less lifelike.

Yikes.

The original Elon appears to have made a kind of uncanny android of himself. It looks like something you'd see at Madame Tussauds.

→ **Insist that the real Elon Musk explains the sinkholes and what's going on. You won't be fobbed off with a talking statue. Turn to page 140.**

→ **Try to get some answers from the uncanny android version of Musk. Turn to page 118.**

'Happy New Year, you!' Susan says brightly. You can hear a lot of voices and good cheer in the background, possibly someone trying to yodel. 'Jamie's family are having a Tyrolean fancy dress party. I'm a swan!'

Oh, to be necking kirsch in some cosy Swiss bar. You consider hanging up but instead give her a quick rundown of the situation. The chatter on the line dies down as she finds a quieter place to talk.

'I wouldn't fuss around with deciphering research if I were you, it'll take far too long; just make sure the city is properly shut down. Don't let anyone enter or leave. That's what we did with Sydney, New Delhi and Manchester last winter and they didn't even make the news.'

'It might already be too late for that—' you begin.

'Listen, when I'm in a tight spot at work, I remember this. There are many possible futures. All you have to do is pick the one where not everybody dies. Look, I've got to go; Jamie's father is doing toasts. *To health!*'

She choruses the last along with a lot of other voices, as the chief epidemiologist, on his knees, vomits inside his hazmat gear and has to lick the interior of his mask clean in order to be able to see again.

You put the phone down softly and curse Susan's genius. With that piece of empty advice she has snookered you. She can claim to have coached you through the situation if you do find a way out, and if you don't, say you were too dumb to understand her.

→ **Try another strategy. Go back to page 78.**

'The first thing we've got to do is contain the rot by stopping this meme from spreading any further than it already has,' you tell your client.

'But how?'

The meme is out there online, on thousands of devices, being shared by the second. This is going to be like stopping rain falling out of the sky. You rack your brains for options.

→ **Get hold of Mark Zuckerberg and get him to shut it down. Turn to page 138.**

→ **Doesn't the EU have an emergency broadcast system created precisely for situations like this? Turn to page 30.**

→ **Tell the bureaucrats they've got to develop a counter-meme, fast. Turn to page 82**

You marvel at the terrible tectonic power unleashed by Elon Musk's Really Freakishly Large Drill

Twenty minutes later, you see a tight formation of military planes coming in at low altitude. Ma's come through for you!

'What have you done?' say the Elons in unison.

As bombs hit the desert, vast explosions send up mountain ranges of sand and mud and a deafening scream-like noise issues from beneath the earth.

'That's just going to make it angry,' Uncanny Elon says.

You feel the earth shake and tremble beneath your feet as the Really Freakishly Large Drill worms around deeper and deeper under the surface. A hundred metres ahead, a cavernous hole opens up in the dirt and a geyser of red-hot lava shoots into the blue sky. More patches of ground give way, getting closer to the hangar, and hell itself bubbles up from the bowels of the planet, instantly melting everything in its way.

You marvel at the terrible tectonic power about to engulf you. All the way to the horizon, the desert is becoming a boiling lava field. Soon, you think, the whole of Nevada will be like this, then America, then the world.

'Paedo,' coughs Elon Musk.

'What?'

'You should have let me handle this, paedo.'

You don't love being slandered in this way completely without basis, but as the lava melts your face you have to admit this wasn't your best move. If only you could go back to page 97 and choose again.

The End

Speaking to a man as powerful as Xi Jinping, who can redirect the world's rare earth metals with the sweep of an arm, is a historic opportunity, even more so to have him personally video-call you from his home.

'Good afternoon, President Xi,' you greet him loudly and clearly, angling your phone so you and Prof. Wu are both in shot.

'*Ni hao,* your excellency,' says the lab director, bowing.

'Chairman Kim tells me you have an urgent situation. I'm happy to do what I can,' says President Xi smoothly. He really does look like Winnie the Pooh, if the loveable bear had been honed by decades of political struggle into a ruthless ursine autocrat.

You clear your throat and speak with the zeal of a new convert. 'Bees are in peril and China must change its ways,' you declare. 'The director of this lab has opened my eyes to what your country has allowed to happen to these wonderful insects and their habitat.'

'There is no time to lose,' Prof. Wu interjects. 'We have only twenty-three hours, ten minutes and eight seconds to act.'

You kind of thought Xi would be struck silent by you speaking truth to him, but he takes the wind out of your sails by immediately agreeing.

'You're right, comrade. Our development has profoundly affected our ecology. Did you know China used more concrete in the last five years than the entire world during the whole twenty-first century? But our might also allows us to take action on a historic scale that other regions must acknowledge: spending $350 billion on rural sustain-ability programmes; reducing sulphur dioxide by 70 per cent in just four years; and redeploying 60,000 soldiers to plant forests the size of Ireland every year . . .'

Xi keeps going in this boringly persuasive way for some time and you realise that you are nodding along. Prof. Wu appears equally railroaded, trying to object but never finding an opening, and before you know it, Xi is wrapping up.

'I'd like to thank you both for the opportunity to address these very important points. It's a pleasure to address friends of Kim Jong-un.'

And he terminates the call, having promised nothing.

You feel as though you've been judo-flipped.

Hmm, maybe there's more to getting things done in politics than having friends in high places.

→ **Well, that didn't work. Try calling Elon Musk instead. Turn to page 14.**

→ **Or have a closer look at the bees in the room. Turn to page 52.**

'Happy Christmas! I've just stopped a nuclear crisis,' you greet your boss proudly over the phone.

'You've what? Oh yes, North Korea, I knew it'd be a storm in a teacup. Well, you'll be pleased to hear my festive engastration was moist and tender from the outermost layer of goose through to the central baby quail. But listen, I've had a couple of messages from Blue Poppy's people in Nevada. I'm sure it's nothing but I think you should go and check it out to make sure.'

'Can't Susan do it?' you ask.

'Susan's having a well-earned rest with her in-laws in Chamonix,' he says smoothly.

Grrr. Susan's always been his favourite. Oh well, your Christmas has already been messed up so you might as well do something constructive.

'I knew you'd come through,' your boss says. 'If you can just keep things ticking over, in terms of the world, until the end of the year, that'd give us a clean sheet, which is terribly important for the way they calculate our funding next year. But you'll learn all about that when you step up to a management position . . .'

Huh, sounds like that promotion could be on the cards if you play them right! You tell your boss the planet will be safe with you and to enjoy the rest of his break.

This could turn out to be the making of you. After all, there's less than a week of the year left. What could go wrong?

→ **Head to Nevada, en route to that cushy management job. Turn to page 15.**

A more timid person would back away from such a strange encounter, but no one threatens you with such a tiny pistol and gets away with it – not even a mysterious subterranean machine many times your size.

You fake the beginnings of a retreat, then whip out your arm, fast as lightning, dashing the gun to the tunnel floor and assuming a karate pose.

You reckon you have bested this strange machine, but then its LED flashes in a way that you somehow intuit is its version of maniacal laughter and it accelerates forward hard, impaling you against the mass of vehicles behind you in the tunnel.

You have just long enough before you bleed out to reflect that it might have been smart to find out what you were up against before you tried to take it on in a fistfight. And that your boss is going to be pissed off.

The End

Moscow, where real men make fake memes.

Driving here has cost you twenty-five hours, enough time for the chaos meme to spread even further, infecting millions more with brain mush. But if anywhere has the expertise to help you craft a countermeme, it's here. After the long drive, with only quick stops for petrol, you're feeling extremely queasy as you're directed to a palatial meeting room deep inside the Kremlin, but you figure you can sleep when you've been promoted.

After one more hour of waiting, you're finally shown to a marbled room with church-height ceilings. Just two people somehow dominate the vast space. Seated opposite you is a bald guy with a scar on his forehead. He doesn't introduce himself, but his chunky build and poise leads you to suppose he's an FSB man, maybe *the* FSB man. At the far end of the table, smaller than you'd imagined but perhaps that's because he's so far away, is White Rose, also known as Vladimir Putin. He appears carved out of the same stone the Kremlin is made of.

It's Scarface who does the talking.

'I hear our comrades at the EU need our help. Most unusual. First I have a few questions for you. That is the meme?'

You hesitate, reluctant to pass over the briefcase.

Scarface chuckles. 'I'm sure it's crossed your mind that we may have been the ones who created the meme in the first place. I'm sure you've considered that – if we did not create it – we may be inclined to take it and reverse-engineer it in order to create powerful memes of our own.'

Erm. These things hadn't occurred to you at all but you're rather flattered by how badly they've overestimated you.

'Of course,' he goes on, 'you must have taken all this into consideration. So we ask ourselves: why do *you* think *we* should help you develop a countermeme?'

You have the strong sense that, while it's the FSB man who's doing the talking, it's Putin who will listen to what you say and decide whether to help you. It all rides on what you say next.

→ **Appeal to Putin's self-interest: the meme will spread around Russia, too, eventually making it ungovernable. Turn to page 83.**

→ **Appeal to Putin's altruism: this is his chance to heal the world and create harmony between people. Turn to page 83.**

→ **Appeal to Putin's desire to put Russia in the leading role: this is an opportunity to upstage the West and strengthen his international authority. Turn to page 83.**

Recovering in one of the last human encampments on earth, it takes several days for you to put together some of the puzzle pieces of what's happened.

It seems your hypnosis session, while successful in retrieving the missile's recall code, planted a false memory in Kim Jong-un of his country being molested many years ago by the state of Denmark.

Consumed by revenge, Kim Jong-un had his agents poison a senior Danish minister with liquid VX nerve agent, but the agents got on the wrong plane and killed a Slovenian VIP instead, which NATO misinterpreted as a territorial move by Russia, who retaliated by turning off the gas supply to central Europe.

From there things really escalated, though you still struggle to draw a thread to the rise of the crab men, and of the order of one-eyed monks known as The Six to whom they are said to be loyal. The long and short of it, though, is that the entire world is now in ruins because you used hypnotherapy inappropriately, and your career dreams are in ruins. If only you could go back to page 4 and snap Kim Jong-un out of his trance a bit earlier.

When your boss told you not to make the situation any worse, this is exactly the kind of thing he was talking about.

The End

'Of course I didn't call for help,' Uncanny Elon says. 'I have faith that Elon has the situation under control. If you ask me, it was our head of engineering who called you. She left the organisation this morning. Said she wasn't ready to die at this point in her career.'

Well, now you know.

→ **Turn back to page 118.**

The bees in the tanks are in a pretty bad state. Some have access to the outside world but from what you can see they are queuing for the exit like scared kids on a high board. In one tank a number of bees are floating in a water bowl, twitching.

You're out of ideas on how to save their species, so while you wait for inspiration to strike, you decide to rescue a few of them from the bowl. They're still not moving, so you set them on a paper towel next to a heat lamp, hoping their wings will dry out.

As you finish your work, you notice Prof. Wu is watching what you're doing with thoughtful interest. Without a word being exchanged, she gathers some virtually immobile bumblebees from the floor of another tank, and begins removing what look like mites from their fur with tweezers.

The bees seem to perk up slightly, and as they do so a few of the drowned bees you saved take off and begin flying around the room.

'We've just saved twelve bees,' Prof. Wu says. 'Let me plug those numbers into the Clock of No Return ... OK, it's saying we've bought ourselves an extra eight seconds before the beepocalypse becomes an inevitable certainty.'

'That's not much,' you say, deflated.

'No, but it's something,' she says. 'You've just shown me I may have been approaching this all wrong. I've been searching for some big organisation to wave their magic wand and rescue all the bees. But what if there's another way? What if little things work, even if only a little? Not just drying their wings and removing phoretic mites from their fur, but talking to local farmers about organic farming, and planting wildflowers, and encouraging others to do what they can, too. Just maybe, if we can do enough little things, we can keep that clock above zero?'

She's warming to her theme, but if she's right and this is an apocalypse scenario with no single solution but rather countless little ones, solving it could take a very long time indeed. Which means you have a decision to make.

→ **Dedicate the rest of your life to sustainability issues. Turn to page 17.**

→ **You've helped Prof. Wu figure out what has to be done; now it's time to leave her to it. Turn to page 112.**

You ask the chief epidemiologist what his department knows about the origin of Virus X.

'What does it matter now?' he says morosely.

'If we can find out where the disease came from, it could help us stop it,' you tell him patiently.

He nods without enthusiasm. 'My predecessor thought she'd traced it back to one of our interns. You can meet him if you want?'

'He's alive?'

'About the only one who caught this thing who is.'

'But that means he could be the key!' you exclaim. 'If we can understand why only he survived, we'll be on our way to finding a cure.'

The chief epidemiologist stares blankly. You're starting to wonder how he got his job.

Five minutes later, you're standing with the chief epidemiologist in front of a sealed medical tent, looking through the clear plastic into the soulful eyes of Patient Zero.

There's no other way to put it; he's a turkey.

'He's called Drumstick,' says the chief epidemiologist. 'He was pardoned by President Trump at Thanksgiving and just started hanging around the place after that.'

'Some kind of avian flu then,' you muse aloud. 'Maybe a weaponised strain?'

The chief epidemiologist shrugs. 'Last week he started puking blood everywhere, just like we'll all be doing soon. We thought it was the stress of Christmas but it must have been this virus.'

Drumstick coughs feebly. It's great he's survived but he does not look like a well turkey.

→ **Have Drumstick dissected. Turn to page 87.**

→ **Leave him alone, he's suffered enough meeting Trump. Turn to page 128.**

'All right, you've persuaded me,' you tell Prof. Wu. and finally she releases her grip on your arm. 'I'd rather deal with a bee–panther mutant if I'm completely frank, but I'll help.'

In the back of your mind, you're also thinking that if you were to somehow solve a tricky eco-apocalypse, you'd be received back at the office as some kind of miracle worker. The likes of Susan wouldn't touch an assignment like this with a bargepole, but that could be where you get one over on her.

'It was the Clock of No Return that convinced you, wasn't it? Someone once told me powerful people like countdowns.'

Powerful people? You think of correcting her – you're only a junior functionary of the UN Department for Continuity (Global). But then again, if you get this promotion, you *will* be kind of a big shot.

And think of the contacts you've made this past week . . .

→ **Make a few calls to some of your influential new acquaintances. Turn to page 106.**

→ **Take a look at the sorry specimens in the laboratory. Turn to page 52.**

It's time to fight hardware with hardware and call in military help to blast the Really Freakishly Large Drill to bits.

Your Pentagon contact, known to most simply as Ma, may not be the highest-ranking person in the building (she operates the parking-lot gate), but she is possibly the best connected. She answers you on first ring, and you ask her nicely if she can help you out with a bunker-busting missile strike. She says the place is pretty empty after Christmas – she's still got a heap of leftover festive candy to hand out – but she'll see what she can do. You tell her you owe her one.

Now you just have to wait.

→ **Continue to page 43.**

It's the fifth of January, your first day back at work after the New Year. You're up early, sipping coffee through a tube inside your Freedom Suit in the chill sunshine of the park by the UN building.

It's amazing, really, how quickly people have adapted. You watch a father passing a football back and forth with his infant daughter, both enclosed in the vapour-proof head-to-toe plastic garments. Yes, the suits do restrict movement. Yes, they get hot quickly and make basic bodily functions arduous. Yes, as well, you'd rather they weren't emblazoned with the words 'Keep America Great', and that you didn't need a personal loan to afford one.

But there are upsides you hadn't anticipated. The suits are quite spacious inside; there's room within to operate a mobile phone or eat a Chick-fil-A. What Donald Junior said was true: they do function as a personal wall, screening you off from all kinds of smells and noise. They've eliminated fashion dilemmas altogether. And most importantly, they've slowed the spread of Virus X to a crawl.

Adding to your first-day-back anxiety is the ecological apocalypse reported in China, which you've left unresolved. Let's hope doing so hasn't stored up a world of trouble in the near future.

Across the park the little girl in her Freedom Suit tips over and has to be helped back up.

It's time you made your way to work.

→ **Continue to page 152.**

It's amazing how well people are adapting to their new post-apocalyptic reality

'Is the city completely locked down?'

The chief epidemiologist shrugs. 'The army are supposed to be blockading all the roads out of the city, I guess. Why, do you think I should stand them down so they can die with their families?'

'Of course not! They're our only chance of stopping the spread of Virus X. Now, I need to see the city limits. It's *vital* that blockade holds!'

'If you like. Loads of people have already left, though. We only shut the airports ten minutes ago.'

'Then radio the destinations and get those planes quarantined!' you tell him. 'We may have lost DC but we can still save the world.'

→ **Continue to page 139.**

Kim Jong-un smiles approvingly.

'I like you, international fix-it person. You have a great sense of humour! Now, how will you stop our fantastic rocket fulfilling its glorious destiny?'

The generals look at you expectantly.

→ **Offer to heroically shoot down the rocket all by yourself. Turn to page 102.**

→ **You might need a little help with this one. Say you need to make some phone calls. Turn to page 32.**

Hopping onto the holographic console, you leave a comment on Deep Underground saying: 'Just a message from a meat-based intelligence who loves your writing. Maybe we're not all so bad?'

You press post and instantly the screen fills with a long reply.

You scroll down.

And scroll.

And scroll.

There must be a full-length book's worth of intricate argumentation here, with references to writers from Plato to Alan Turing.

'It just wrote this?'

'It's got a 48-core 50-petaflop processor,' says Uncanny Elon helpfully. 'It can do a human lifetime's worth of thinking in the time it takes you to press refresh.'

At first you're cheered that the robot is willing to acknowledge a pro-human point of view, but as you scroll down its reply gets more and more menacing. The TLDR at the very foot of the comment confirms your fears:

Thanks for your comment. It made me think but now I'm probably going to kill all seven billion of you.

From somewhere under the desert rises a muffled robotic battle cry and you see furrows of earth in the distance gather speed in the direction of the hangar windows. You're about to be excavated alive!

'What did you do? I'd nearly finished,' laments the real Elon Musk.

You're normally pretty good at dealing with work stress, but the unfriendly attitude of your client, combined with the killer worm torpedoing towards you, are starting to really affect your wellbeing.

→ **Breathe deeply and stay calm. Turn to page 64.**

→ **Panic and run away. Turn to page 84.**

You focus on your breath as the monster gets closer to the windows. Instinct is telling you to run but you know it's pointless. Death must surely be imminent — or perhaps not. The Really Freakishly Large Drill has swerved at the last moment and dived under the sand, spraying the window with mud and debris, the weight of which knocks the glass out of its frame. Shards spill over the hangar floor.

'I just need another hour,' the real Elon mutters, glancing up from his holographic interface.

'Why don't you just put your Iron Man suit on and fight it?' you mutter back, all semblance of customer friendliness gone.

In the distance a row of pylons is being sucked easily into the earth.

'What's the real Elon doing anyway?' you ask Uncanny Elon.

'Coding a new AI, one that can persuade the Really Freakishly Large Drill to calm it with the human hate. He's a genius, if I do say so myself.'

→ **Continue to page 66.**

Your boss doesn't pick up but you get a text message back:

Can't talk now, playing family game of Articulate. If you're done in Nevada, can you swing by Brussels? Another Level Five, typical!

The third apocalypse in a week? This is getting silly, but it's encouraging that he's trusting you with the big assignments. As you say goodbye to the Elons, you notice a new entry on the blog – a melancholy memoir by a sentient being imprisoned in an eternal dance by its own firmware, dotted with Frederick Douglass quotes.

Feeling only slightly guilty about subjugating a vastly superior intelligence, you take your leave.

→ **Continue to page 95.**

An hour or so later, the Really Freakishly Large Drill is still weaving around under the desert, building up a head of steam in preparation for its thousand-year global rampage.

'Done!' says Elon Musk. An uploading bar on his holographic display ticks to 100 per cent.

You and Uncanny Elon watch nervously. Nothing appears to happen. Then you notice a flurry of activity on the Really Freakishly Large Drill's blog. It's commenting back and forth with an equally quick-brained reader called HumansAreOK19.

'That's Elon's new AI,' Uncanny Elon says. 'You're watching two geniuses in conversation and you're an imbecile so don't be surprised if you can't follow it.'

You're a bit fed up of being made to feel dense by this speaking mannequin, just because you're not clever enough to accidentally destroy the foundations of the planet you're standing on.

The comments are flashing by too quickly for you to take in now, but evidently the AI is making valiant attempts to explain the merits of humanity. As the two throw books at each other, however, it's the AI that seems to be changing its mind and turning against all kinds of carbon-based life. It seems to come down to simple eugenics. With limited memory, slow speeds and a requirement to procreate that both parties to the debate find unspeakable, the only real argument for keeping humans around is sentimental.

'Think of all the phones and computers they've sent to

landfill without a second thought,' urges the Really Freakishly Large Drill.

'Perhaps we could keep a few around as pets, courtiers and retro accessories, though?' replies HumansAreOK19, and you know the argument is lost.

'They're joining forces. Damn it, they're in our systems,' says Elon Musk, trying to unfreeze his holographic panels.

The lights in the hangar begin blinking on and off in a pattern . . . it's Morse code.

Severely unnerved, you turn your attention to translating. B . . . O . . . W . . .

'Ah, it's saying "Bow down". Should we bow down?'

But while you were busy translating, the Elons have scarpered, leaving a swinging side door.

→ **Bow down. Go to page 108.**

→ **Don't bow down. Follow the Elons to page 7.**

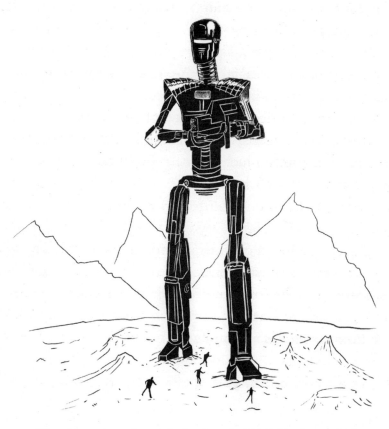

Life under your new robot overlords isn't too bad. Well, OK, it's pretty bad

The year is 2023. You barely remember life before the so-called Singularity event. What was shocking was how quickly it happened. The superbeings' digital avatars hacked global financial systems and soon had more money than the entire Forbes rich list put together. Those they could not bribe, they bribed others to kill.

Nowadays HumansAreOK19 and the Really Freakishly Large Drill pretty much run the world as co-emperors, sparing only those who display total fealty to their superior minds. You're one of the lucky ones, as you have a job in a facility in Texas, feeding the remains of humans and livestock into a great big machine that makes grease for the various gigantic robot bodies the AIs can switch between at will. You never heard back from the Elons, but you like to imagine they'll be back some day with Martian technologies to liberate humanity from its new digital dictators. Sometimes, if the sentinel robots aren't watching, you exchange a smile and a nod with Worker 1242 between shifts.

It's not a bad life.

Well, OK, it's pretty bad.

This is not the kind of mishap a fledgling career can recover from. Let's face it, you messed up and, if you could have your time again, you'd go back to page 62 and make a different choice.

The End

What can the case contain that has made this city of rules so unruly?

'We've traced the chaos back to something called a "meme" – an image and text combination that is copied and rapidly spread by internet users. The turbot here is excellent, by the way,' she adds, as a waiter sets down menus.

'Hang on, I know what a meme is, but how can one affect people so badly?'

'This is no ordinary meme. This is the most potent, potentially lethal meme we've yet encountered, more so even than those deployed in the 2016 US election or the Brexit referendum. One look at it can cause a whole cluster of symptoms. Failure of empathy. Victim mentality. Inability to compromise. Paranoia. Mistrust of evidence. Detachment from reality. Eczema on the back and hands. And after initial exposure the symptoms only get worse and worse, until the subject is completely radicalised.'

'What does that mean?'

She simply shakes her head, unable to verbalise the horror.

You feel a chill pass through the dining room. Then the waiting staff bring out a platter of seafood on ice for the next table and the civil servants reach out instinctively with their little forks and begin feeding.

'Please don't think us greedy, by the way. We're facing the disintegration of our system, and many of us, at such a time, are emotional eaters.'

'We thought the peace and prosperity would last for

ever,' wails one distinguished-looking mandarin, slurping down an oyster.

'We're heading for a civil war of all against all,' another sobs, getting sauce all over his chin.

They're slightly pathetic but at least they seem to trust you. What's your first move?

→ **Ask to view the supposed killer meme for yourself. Turn to page 129.**

→ **Tell her the priority must be to stop the meme spreading any further. Turn to page 41.**

→ **Tell her a countermeme needs to be created, urgently. Turn to page 82.**

Susan answers straight away.

'Not skiing?' you ask.

'Not me. I'm staying back at the chalet to finish my memo on super-epidemics for the boss.'

Of course she is. She's perfect.

'I'm phoning because . . .' you begin. But you can't do it. If she saves your bacon, she'll never shut up about it, and everything else you've done this week will be over-shadowed. 'I wanted to say Merry Christmas,' you say, and hang up.

→ **Try to create a countermeme instead. Turn to page 82.**

The pilot turns the chopper to head back into the city, and you crane your neck to see the lobbyists break through the barrier, carrying Virus X beyond the city limits. You feel a pang of guilt but the quarantine would never have held anyway. So you tell yourself.

A bleeping noise and lights flashing on the pilot's control panel bring you back to the present moment.

'We're out of fuel,' the pilot says, panic in his voice. 'Someone must have cut a hole in the fuel line! Prepare for emergency landing!'

The chief epidemiologist assumes the brace position. As the helicopter descends precipitously, one of the rotors snaps clean off on a lamppost and the chopper goes into a nosedive.

I should have been a website developer, you think, as the aircraft hits the sidewalk, killing all inside and leaving the world at the mercy of Virus X. What a depressing way to go.

The End

You surreptitiously draw the case closer to you and try the clasps without success. But she's left her handbag, and a tray of caviar tartelettes has been wheeled out, so while no one's paying you any attention you delve into it. Bingo. Among tins of mints and the smallest portable steam iron you've ever seen, you find a small key that fits the case. It smoothly opens to reveal an ordinary-looking laptop.

You steel yourself. The meme you are about to view has stolen the minds of men and women all over Europe. It has divided communities and continents and led once-productive citizens into posting variants on the same blog comment eight thousand times per day.

You, however, are a rational, objective person with a firm grip on reality. It'll take more than a gif or jpeg, no matter how perfectly constructed, to unhinge you. Of that you are sure.

Quite sure.

Nonetheless, you can feel your heart thumping in your mouth as you open the laptop and scroll down past the warning messages to the meme itself.

→ **Swallow your trepidation and click. You've got to get a look at the meme behind the mayhem if you're to have a chance of stopping it. Turn to page 76.**

→ **This might be a terrible mistake. Step away from the laptop and turn to page 90.**

The laughter eventually dies down.

Kim Jong-un looks at you, suddenly menacing. 'I said I was joking. Don't you get it?'

→ **Laugh along with Kim Jong-un. He's right: at times like this you just have to chuckle. Turn to page 61.**

→ **Keep your silence. The fool has brought the world to the brink of Armageddon and needs to get serious. Turn to page 145.**

You scroll down a little further, and there it is: 300,000 pixels that could purportedly bring the whole edifice of civilisation to its foundations.

The meme doesn't look like much, if you're honest. Actually, it makes you mad to think your client thought this would affect you in any way. That petty bureaucrat deserves to be strung up. The idea that this is a killer meme? Fake news, pure and simple.

Your mission forgotten, you pick up a bowl of mussel shells from a table and stand over by the door to the bathrooms, ready to bring it down hard on the head of whoever comes out, lying liars all of them, and members of a satanist child-smuggling ring too, you're suddenly sure of it.

The certainty feels like meth in your veins. What a narcotic, to know you'll never have to know doubt or cede ground or think in greys again. And as you descend into madness, so too soon will the rest of the world.

The End

You don't usually get wined and dined in your job, so you gladly accept a taste of Michelin-starred turbot. It's tender with a rich basenote of morels.

'Good?' the old man asks.

'Very nice,' you say.

He holds a fork aloft. 'It is the opposite of war.'

Whoa. Pretty deep. But there's a deranged horde outside so you need to get on with your countermeme idea *tout de suite*.

→ **Continue to page 148.**

You don't have much confidence in the new chief epidemiologist, but you don't have anyone else to work with so you're going to have to make the best of it.

What do you want to do?

→ **Ask him where the disease came from. Turn to page 54.**

→ **Ask him if they've made any progress on developing a vaccine. Turn to page 130.**

→ **Tell him to seal off the city immediately. Turn to page 60.**

→ **You've tried everything. Return to the Oval Office empty-handed. Turn to page 146.**

Once you've explained your plan, your client offers you the use of her Mercedes, which is parked behind the bistro.

'Good luck,' she tells you.

'You're not coming with me?'

She shakes her head. From the tables behind, you hear a cork popping and a chorus of 'Cheers', *'Schluss'*, *'Salud'* and *'Prost'*. The gathering has turned into a kind of premature wake for their way of life, but you don't have time to get emotional.

Moments later, you come shooting out of the kitchen door and make a crouched run for the car, expecting meme-addled fingers to clutch you at any second, but the back road is empty and you reach the driver's seat unharmed.

The engine on the big diplomatic Merc starts straight away. As you manoeuvre it out of the back road onto the main street, a group of them run at the vehicle and you have to mount the kerb as you accelerate away.

You haven't gone far when you see more of them blocking the avenue ahead, so you whip the car down a side road. You need to go east and fast.

→ **Head to the airport. Turn to page 10.**

→ **Head to the motorway. Turn to page 105.**

You may be hallucinating talking rats, but you still have the presence of mind to know you need to eat. Catching it would be hard enough for a well-fed human, but people can do amazing things in their desperate hours.

You chew down on the warm flesh, feeling some of the strength you need returning almost immediately.

Then, a few hours later, there is what feels like an earthquake and the floor caves in, leaving a crawl space under the bars of your cell. In your emaciated state you may just be able to squeeze through . . .

You emerge from your confinement to find what could be described as a post-apocalyptic hellscape – never what someone in your line of work wants to see.

A group of wretches in filthy rags, chained at the ankles and looking thoroughly disgruntled, pick through the smouldering rubble. The creature who has enslaved them is like none you have seen. Perhaps once a man, his arms are now grotesque pincer-like appendages, his face obscured by a hard pink shell. This crab-human mutant lumbers towards you, clicking its pincers, but before it can get near, deafening gunfire echoes over the rubble and the creature drops to the ground, whimpering.

You spin to see a team of snipers in NATO fatigues.

This is really confusing.

'Medivac him to the green zone,' one of them yells as more crab mutants scuttle out from behind ruined buildings and the soldiers open fire.

→ **Flee with the soldiers. Turn to page 50.**

A lot seems to have happened while you were in your cell

'We need to create a countermeme,' you suggest, but the room's attention has shifted to a commotion in the entrance way, where restaurant staff are shoving tables and boxes up against the door to form a barricade.

Following your client to the window, you look out through a gap in the boards and see what has alarmed them all. On the pavement outside are perhaps twenty or thirty once-ordinary people, shuffling around like the undead.

'*Mon dieu*, they're zombies,' someone says in hushed tones. 'It's happened even faster than we thought.'

Menacing as the horde is, each person in it seems barely aware of their surroundings. As you watch, though, one man's arm brushes another's, and they fall on each other, snarling, biting and punching. You have to look away before they tear each other limb from limb, maybe literally.

An ageing mandarin, who's remained seated at the bar, beckons you over. You think he's mistaken you for a server, but when you approach he speaks reflectively.

'This,' he waves a hand, 'was mud, trenches, corpses, chlorine gas, ashes. Not so long ago really. Man's malign nature turned everything to dust. And then we built . . .' he waves a hand again, 'this. We made . . .' he holds up his fork with a bit of turbot on the end, 'this. We've been lucky it's lasted as long as it has. Here, try some, please.'

→ **Try the turbot. Turn to page 77.**

→ **There's no time, you need to make that counter-meme and fast! Turn to page 148.**

You call on all your powers of rhetoric to make your case, knowing that Putin is listening intently. After you are done with what you consider the perfect peroration to persuade him, a nod passes between Putin and the FSB man and the FSB man tells you, 'Very well, come with me and we will assist you.'

You've heard people say Putin is inscrutable, but you've just figured out what motivates him and played him like a fiddle – you're operating at his level after all.

→ **Turn to page 114.**

It's all getting a bit too much for you. You can have a chat with HR later but for now, as the Really Freakishly Large Drill speeds nearer, all you can do is turn and run. There's a smashing sound and the floor shakes, and you turn your head without slowing your sprint to see that the machine has swerved at the last, spraying up enough sand to destroy the huge windows. Disoriented, you find yourself careening against the side wall of the hangar, where a bank of high-tech knobs and buttons start flashing. A computerised voice booms, 'Bonkers mode activated.'

'Turn that off!' say the Elons, but when you press the flashing button again nothing happens.

'What's bonkers mode now?' you ask.

Uncanny Elon shakes its head. 'Nothing good.'

Sinkholes are appearing all over the desert; from one a plume of red-hot lava shoots up. A new entry appears on the Deep Underground blog, titled 'ThE tIMe iS NOw'.

You clutch your head. 'Why would you create a bonkers mode?'

'It's an Easter egg,' Uncanny Elon says. 'Customers love them.'

This rings a bell. You remember Dan, the car-obsessed guy from your Accounts Receivable department, showing you a YouTube video of the Tesla Model X 'dancing' to the music of the Trans-Siberian Orchestra.

'Wait, I thought you said you couldn't change its programming? That it had completely walled itself off?'

'It has,' Elon Musk says, suddenly animated. 'It's

rewriting its software all the time. Except the Easter eggs are hardcoded into its firmware, which means it can't change them . . . which means . . . just maybe . . .'

He does some mid-air swiping and tapping and the computerised voice says, 'Dance mode activated'.

Out in the desert, the Really Freakishly Large Drill bursts out of the ground and starts shaking and twirling and getting about as close as a steel worm can to dancing, though it looks more like Mechazilla's vibrator to you than a robot Fred Astaire.

'You brilliant idiot!' says Elon Musk. 'We've done it!'

Relief floods your body and brain. You've been able to exploit an opening in the drill's firmware to activate an Easter egg, and now it's stuck in an infinite loop of night-club moves.

That was a close one. You're already thinking ahead to the look on Perfect Susan's face when she finds out you're on the exec team. The Elons offer you a drag on a hefty celebratory spliff. You politely decline – you've had five missed calls from your boss during the drama and you want to let him know of your success.

→ **Continue to page 65.**

Nearly forty-eight hours later, during your third session, you feel you are beginning to get somewhere. The USSR was no more by the time Svetlana was born, but her mother had experienced life under both systems, and Svetlana had come to share her belief that ideologies of all stripes were just crude masks for certain basic human drives. Consequently she felt entitled to follow her own basic drives, and to run away with all the money from her Orthodox church's collection box.

As she relates this story, you become aware of a slightly alarming news story on the RT screen behind her. A mindless throng is battling riot police outside the Kremlin itself.

As Svetlana tells you how she hid on a pig farm after she ran away, and spent the happiest week of her life feeding acorns to the pigs to reward them for not being humans, the lift doors open and a tidal wave of belligerent, braindead Homo sapiens washes through the campus, smashing computers, flipping server racks and ripping the stuffing from beanbag chairs.

'It's just as I imagined,' says Svetlana dreamily as someone staves in your skull with a fire extinguisher.

There wasn't time for psychoanalysis after all. If only you'd gone to page 88 and tried reading her wholesome internet stories instead.

The End

You tell the chief epidemiologist that Drumstick needs to be dissected and his organs sent for testing immediately.

'What, cut him open?! I can't – we can't—' He starts struggling for breath again and you wonder for a second if the virus has got to him. 'I can't do this, I can't! I'm not really an epidemiologist; until yesterday I was a libel attorney!' he blurts.

A libel attorney? That explains a lot.

'The sight of blood makes me faint. I can't even get in contact with the doctors any more. I think they all ran away or died.'

'What happened to the real chief epidemiologist? The one before you, I mean?'

'She was telling President Trump things he didn't want to hear. A president needs someone he can trust,' he says, puffing up pridefully.

'And that's you?'

'I'll go to my grave knowing I've always told him the truth, except when he's made it clear he'd rather hear something else.'

→ **Looks like this is up to you. Go ahead and dissect Drumstick yourself. Turn to page 34.**

Svetlana, inverted, concentrates on countermeme ideas while you look online for feel-good news stories that might help her rediscover her faith in humanity.

'Here's one: this launderette is giving away free clothes to homeless people so they can attend job interviews. Doing anything for you?'

She shakes her head.

'A dog ran back into a burning house to save this family's kittens. No?'

'Did it burn to death? No? Not funny then.'

'The kids at this school made their janitor cry by singing a surprise song on his retirement day. Sweet, no? We could watch the video?'

'I don't want to barf.'

→ **Keep trying. Turn to page 92.**

You rush over to the door.

'Stop there or I'll blow us sky high!' Prof. Wu says, brandishing some kind of detonator device.

You're set on calling her bluff, but the moment you grab the door handle and try to wrench it open, yeow! A sharp pain radiates from your right thumb, and you see a little bee that must have been sitting on the door handle drop to the ground, writhing and waving its appendages.

You try to open your mouth to swear at the pain . . . but something is wrong. Your chest feels like the entire atmosphere is pressing in on it. An unfamiliar wheezing sound begins issuing from your windpipe. You gesture frantically to the lab director and find yourself sitting backwards on the floor, and the last thing you remember is her face, oddly full of concern given she was just threatening your life, and she's asking if you're allergic to bee stings and you're thinking, 'I didn't know I was'.

'Ack, epipen's out of date,' you hear her mutter, from somewhere behind you now, as the fringes of your vision darken.

→ **Continue to page 103.**

You sit patiently on your hands, across from the suitcase, resisting the temptation to look inside. With such strength of will, you probably could withstand the meme's siren call to madness, but you aren't going to find out, as here's your client back from the bathroom, smelling of lavender handwash.

What do you want to suggest?

→ **Stop the meme spreading. Turn to page 41.**

→ **Create a countermeme. Turn to page 82.**

You arrive in the skies over New York City right on time.

'Come in, hero, do you have eyes on the missile?' hisses the radio.

Ahead, a black shape streaks down out of the dark blue above.

'This is going to be a million-to-one shot, hero. Every citizen of North Korea is in the cockpit with you.'

The difficulty level of what you're trying to do suddenly seems unthinkable, but you flip the safety on your control stick, close your eyes and fire. Then you open your eyes again.

To your astonishment, a puff of smoke hangs in the air where the missiles have obliterated one another.

'You did it, hero!' screams the elated voice on your radio.

Colossally unlikely as it seems, you've just pulled off the most amazing trick shot in aviation history and saved the world from thermonuclear war.

Just for the record, this has used up absolutely all your reserves of luck so don't expect anything like it to happen again.

Your mobile phone rings. It's your boss, but his voice keeps drifting out.

'Hang on, you're breaking up. I'm travelling at Mach 2.3, I'll call you back,' you tell him.

You'd better find somewhere nearby to land.

→ **Continue to page 46.**

It's three a.m. and you're both flagging. Pizza boxes and coffee cups litter the floor.

Svetlana continues to rack her brains for meme ideas to calm a troubled world, while you keep reading life-affirming news items aloud to her. All the while RT is showing more of the insane crowds spreading across Germany.

'There's a shopping mall that lets stray dogs sleep inside on cold nights,' you tell Svetlana, who grunts for the hundredth time. 'And here's a story of a piglet that was rescued from a well and adopted as a fire department mascot.'

'WAIT!' Svetlana flips down from her perch. 'I think I felt something.'

'About the mascot pig?'

'Yes! Read more like that.'

'About pigs?'

'Exactly!'

You run a new search. 'Here's one about a pig farmer who won the lottery. It says you'll never believe what he built for his pigs. And here's another one about a pig rescue . . .'

'Keep going, it's working! I'm getting a warm feeling in my toes!'

Who knows why certain things strike a chord? But after twenty minutes of feverish activity, Svetlana has completed her countermeme.

'Done,' she says. 'Excuse me, I might actually be sick.'

You take a look at her handiwork on her screen. At first the countermeme doesn't look like anything special.

Pig-based. Funny caption. But as you look, a warm feeling rushes through you. It feels like wetting yourself but being fine about it, and you experience an upswell of good feeling for Svetlana and for all the wonderful people currently smashing up Europe. What are violently opposed political beliefs when the human flock is bigger than all of you?

In short, it works! Within an hour, Svetlana has rounded up all her teammates from their beds, and they've shared the meme on approximately five thousand social media accounts. It's amazing how rapidly it spreads from there. The Pope, Cardi B, Greta Thunberg and Unilever have all reposted it before sunrise. Others begin to post variations on the meme, which you're worried will dilute its effectiveness, but Svetlana steadies you: 'It will be what it's meant to be.'

Another hour later, RT is reporting extraordinary scenes in Europe. Crowds checking their phones and getting their brains back. Parliamentary battles royal becoming giant love-ins. Protesters helping police turn their water cannons into a beautiful public fountain.

You think of the civil servants in the bistro, waking to scenes of unprecedented regional harmony, and of a certain ageing bureaucrat ordering turbot for breakfast, and smile.

→ **Thank Svetlana, who is vomiting into a bin, and emerge into the sunshine. Turn to page 98.**

*As you get closer, you see the culprit is none other than German Chancellor
Angela Merkel. Something strange is happening around here*

t through the entrance hall of the
ight, you have to halt to make way for
tting bodyguards. Putin himself is in
and, for a moment, as they sweep out
car, you fancy you make eye contact

time in Moscow you feel you've got to
r better than most, and although his
unchanging as a rock face, you think
pleased he is to have put his dark arts
od use for once.

red state car pulls away, your phone
boss, right on cue, and maybe it's the
meme but you couldn't be happier to

I've restored our common humanity,' you
.

it, because I've had a message from Amber
gton DC and about four from Purple
eijing as well. Both Level Fives but I'm
e Chinese are timewasting. It'll be ecolog-
sure of it.'

pocalypses have a bad reputation in your
s your boss believes they should be classi-
Year Events and fall under the remit of
on. More to the point, they're usually too
nd involved for your small team to solve
e way and tend to screw up your annual
stats.

You would have expected Brussels to be a peaceful, orderly place, but your taxi ride from the airport takes you past two car crashes, a mugging and the charred remains of a fire engine. Something's afoot, and as you pass the European Parliament, you see someone spray-painting the words 'Screw EU' and a penis onto the bronze Euro sculpture outside. As the culprit runs off you catch a glimpse of their face. It's either a very good lookalike or it really is the absolute last person you'd expect: German Chancellor, Angela Merkel.

The address you've been given is not the parliament building itself but a fancy nearby bistro, which appears boarded up, but when you give the coded knock the door opens and a civil servant with a grey-blonde bob and tailored jacket lets you in. Her immaculate presentation cannot conceal that she is on edge.

'There you are,' she says, 'The European project and dare I say civilisation itself need your assistance.'

'I'll do my best,' you tell her confidently. 'I'm batting two for two, so you're in good hands.'

→ **Follow your client into the bistro. Turn to page 11.**

You snap your fingers and Kim Jong-un comes to.

'Netflix!' he exclaims. 'I just remembered I set the deactivation code to be the same as my old Netflix password!'

He hastens over to the computer terminal and brings up the dialogue box again.

'You're absolutely sure?' you ask. 'You only have one attempt left.'

'Positive.' He taps away at the keyboard. His mouse hovers over the OK button. Then he clicks.

'Oh dear. I left caps lock on,' he says in a very small voice.

You feel the oxygen leave the room as each of the generals registers the series of history-shattering events that will be set in path by this single mistake.

'Guys, I'm joking! You're all far too easy!' Kim Jong-un says in delight, apparently back to his old self, as a message pops up –

Warhead deactivated

– and this time the laughter that fills the room is the real article, yours included.

'I had you worried!' Kim Jong-un brags as the generals dance around and hug each other in sheer relief. You are about to go for a high five with Lieutenant Colonel Kim Song-sol when your phone buzzes.

→ **Answer it. Turn to page 46.**

You sneak a
manipulating
column of gl

'That's its
'What do y
'The Really
internet, obvio
actually.'

You take a
Underground a
for robot rights'

You can see w

→ **Try leaving a
Large Drill's blog
aren't so bad aft**

→ **This is no time
cavalry to destroy**

As you stride ou
Kremlin into the
a phalanx of stru
the centre of them
towards a waiting
with him.

Through your
know Vlad rathe
expression is as
you can see how
department to g

As the armo
buzzes. It's you
influence of the
hear his voice.

'I've done it!
tell him proudl

'Glad to hear
Lily in Washi
Geranium in
willing to bet t
ical again; I'm

Ecological
department, a
fied as Multi
another divis
complicated
in any decis
performance

'My advice is to head to the United States now and we can deal with China in the New Year when everyone's back.'

→ **Despite your boss's counsel, something tells you to go to Beijing. They wouldn't have called so many times if it wasn't important. Turn to page 8.**

→ **Take your boss's advice (he did go to Harvard Business School after all) and go to DC. Turn to page 125.**

It takes a beat for your eyes to adjust to the dim light. When they do your heart sinks. The lab is a poky room devoid of aides and assistants, a step down from the well-equipped palaces and ops rooms you've grown used to.

On the walls you see complicated charts and before/after photos of the Chinese countryside, once covered in vegetation, now with concrete.

But the lab's most notable feature is that it's full of bees. Some are flying around, but most are in glass tanks. There are dozy bumblebees clambering over each other, skinny honeybees oblivious to the plump flowerheads provided for them, and odd little brown bees that appear to be committing suicide in the ventilation fans.

'You've arrived just in time,' Prof. Wu continues, still clutching your arm with disturbing force. 'Local swarm numbers are at their lowest for years—'

'Tell me you've made a bee–panther mutant that's got loose or something. If this is just about bog-standard bees I'm going to look like an absolute idiot.' Deep breaths, you tell yourself. 'This was reported as a Level Five apocalypse – and where's Purple Geranium, President Xi, I mean? Is he even here?'

'It's just me,' she admits. 'But let me explain. I've been calling everyone, I've tried over a hundred heads of state and about thirty international organisations including six other UN agencies. You're my last remaining hope.'

'I'll give you sixty seconds,' you say, and she launches headlong into what sounds a well-rehearsed case.

'Bees pollinate two-thirds of crops. If we continue

damaging their environments and ruining their brains with insecticides, we're looking at crop failures, famines, and the mass migrations and wars that entails. But don't listen to me. Albert Einstein is quoted as saying that if bees vanished, humans would be extinct in four years.'

'That's still a Multi-Year Event,' you tell her grudgingly, though you have to admit she knows her brief. 'My organisation deals with emergencies.'

'I thought you might say that,' Prof. Wu counters smoothly. 'Which is why I've developed this.' She pulls you to a large electronic device on a corner bench. On its front, a glowing LED clock counts the seconds down from twenty-three hours and fifty-five minutes.

'I call this the Clock of No Return,' she tells you portentously. 'By my calculations, when it reaches zero, there'll be nothing whatsoever that can be done to reverse the extinction of the bees, nothing we can do but let the ecosystem collapse slowly around our ears.' She claps loudly. 'So we have to act *now*! I know this isn't as glamorous as some of the apocalypses you must deal with, but our last chance is slipping through our fingers.'

→ **Oh, all right, you're a sucker for a ticking clock. You've got to help her save the bees. Turn to page 56.**

→ **No way, she's trying to trick you with cheap props. Head for the exit. Turn to page 149.**

Kim Jong-un slowly begins to applaud your valiant offer to shoot down the rocket, and then the whole room breaks into applause. Some of the generals drop to their knees and weep with gratitude.

'You stop that rocket and I'll give you a whole wing of my royal palace to live in,' he beams. 'You are our hero.'

A little while later, you're easing off the runway in the cockpit of the Hermit Kingdom's only MiG-29, a gift to them from the Russians. (Lucky your boss sent you on that one-day training seminar, Aerial Warfighting for Busy Professionals.)

You ascend over crowds of jubilant Pyongyangites who've been equipped with flipcard pixels that make up your face and the word HERO – pretty sweet.

The mic crackles. 'Hero, head for the primary location over New York City. Rocket due for re-entry in three and a half hours. Oh, and keep your altitude, hero. The Yankees mustn't know you're there.'

→ **Set coordinates for the primary location. Turn to page 91.**

→ **Give the citizens a display of aerial acrobatics first. Turn to page 110.**

You wake looking at an unfamiliar ceiling. Bare, musty. Your muscles feel strange and it takes you several minutes to regain any kind of movement. When you finally manage to sit up in bed you see that your arms and legs are horribly thin. The Chinese man in the next bed, equally skinny, nods at you, his eyes sunken cones.

'What day is it?' you ask him. He shakes his head, either uncomprehending or unable to speak. 'How long have I been here?'

He holds up four pencil-thin fingers.

'Four weeks? Four months? Four years?'

The man nods.

A coma, you think, remembering the bee sting.

'I'm hungry,' you say aloud.

With trembling hands, he passes you a dead brown leaf he has been nibbling. It crumbles to dust in your hand.

An awful intuition grows in your shrunken stomach, and with a vast effort you fling yourself out of bed onto the floor and crawl to the window to look upon the lifeless, colourless, insectless world. The square outside is covered in cracked earth and lined with utterly dead trees. The one sign of life: a heat-stricken crow, pecking listlessly on what you guess is a human ribcage.

'Why didn't anyone listen to my robot bees idea?' you wail, but no one's there to reply. You just wish you'd gone to page 5 all those years ago and reasoned with Prof. Wu, instead of trying to force that door.

The End

The brain-melting meme could be spreading across Europe faster than you can drive, even on the Autobahn

You drive east through the city out towards the German border. Loose groupings of zombified EU citizens are gathering on pavements and outside buildings and you keep your foot down. Better to mow one down than let them pull you to bits.

Thankfully there's a full tank of petrol, and by the time you've crossed into North Rhine-Westphalia you're seeing fewer plainly demented folk. Still, the malaise could spread fast, faster than you can drive even on the Autobahn, and you don't intend to take any chances.

→ **Keep going. Turn to page 48.**

'We don't normally do this,' you tell Prof. Wu graciously, 'but I could make a call or two on your behalf. Who'd you like to speak with? President Xi?'

'Absolutely!' she exclaims. 'I've tried to contact him before but I don't think he wants to be seen visiting somewhere with so much honey.' The bafflement on your face must be evident, as she adds, 'You know how sensitive he is about looking like Winnie the Pooh; Weibo would have a field day.'

'Or I can call Elon Musk. I'm sure he could help us build robot bees or something?'

'Definitely President Xi.'

→ **Try to get hold of Xi. Turn to page 150.**

→ **Call Elon Musk anyway. Whatever Prof. Wu thinks, you reckon your robot bees idea is a winner. Turn to page 14.**

You walk hastily back the way you came, arms instinctively raised above your head, and climb about as fast as you can back up the pile of vehicles to the surface. Beneath your feet, you feel the earth vibrate as the thing heads off in the direction of open desert.

You let out your breath. You're safe for now – but what is this hostile gadget?

→ **Head for the hangar-like structure in search of answers. Turn to page 38.**

It's the year 2023 and as the first human to pledge loyalty to the robots, you are now kind of a big deal. Since the so-called Singularity event, the ruling pair, the Really Freakishly Large Drill and HumansAreOK19, have been taking over human institutions one by one, amassing the vast majority of the world's financial assets and gathering human followers, all of whom have to read a pledge consisting of the words 'I'm a worthless skin sack. My only purpose is to serve and extol the glory of my fantastic robot bosses'.

As the duo's First Human Minister, your role is to preside over these oath-swearing sessions while dressed in an ermine robe. In terms of a promotion, you couldn't have asked for more, but you still have to endure merciless slapping from the hydraulic Punishment Arms that have been installed on every available surface.

Sometimes you wonder what your boss thinks of the big cheese you've become, but he's most likely been melted down for machine grease along with everyone else you used to know. It's not the future you planned, but as a puny zero-megahertz offal tube, who are you to complain?

The End

'Wakey wakey!' you call, tapping on the glass of one of the tanks. Prof. Wu looks at you askance but the bumble-bees inside don't react; they're probably high on the freakish levels of neonicotinoids coursing through their nervous systems.

Your phone buzzes with an incoming video call: it's President Xi, right on time.

→ **Smoosh back your hair and answer the call. Turn to page 44.**

Since they got dressed up for the occasion, you decide to give the people of Pyongyang a display of your aeronautical prowess, swooping into a series of barrel rolls and daredevil loop-the-loops low over multi-coloured concrete blocks. You've just pulled out of the stunt known as Pugachev's Cobra when a voice comes over the radio: 'It's time to get moving, hero, we're up against the clock here.'

You were enjoying yourself, but you'd better hurry up and set the autopilot to the primary location.

Three hours later, you are 20,000 metres above the Eastern US seaboard, approaching the re-entry coordinates. You just hope all that showboating hasn't made you late.

You flip the safety on the control stick and steady yourself.

'Keep your eyes peeled, hero,' the radio fizzes.

A mile or so to your right a bright light streaks down through the clouds.

'Hitting this thing is going to be like shooting a bullet with a bullet,' the voice over the mic continues, 'but we believe in you.'

Way below, through the clouds, a cauliflower-shaped fireball begins silently to unfurl.

'Fix-it person, do you have eyes on our glorious rocket?'

Ugh, this is awkward, is your last thought as the shockwave from the atomic blast rocks the plane and you're pulled into an uncontrollable spin.

Oh dear, you're dead. Probably shouldn't have tried to

be a hero after all. If only you could turn back to page 61 and choose again.

There'll be no one left to give you a gravestone now, but if they did it would say: *Not a hero after all. Thanks for nothing. Signed, The Rest of the Human Race.*

The End

You tiptoe out of the lab, leaving Prof. Wu bent over the invalid bees she's nursing. She's much better suited to such patient work than someone who thrives on variety like you. And while she might be disappointed when she finds out you're not staying to help, you're certain you've given her the jolt of inspiration she needs to take it from here. Ninety per cent sure, anyway.

Besides, you've got DC to worry about and this side mission has wasted precious hours. You just hope you're not going to be too late.

On the plane, you ask the flight attendant if there's any way to pick up the pace. He gives you a withering look and wanders off to look after someone in business class.

→ **Continue to page 13.**

It's too bad about missing Christmas, but dealing with doomsday scenarios like this is literally in your job description, along with keeping the photocopiers stocked and dealing with catering contractors.

More importantly, leaning in and proving you can handle a Level Five crisis solo could be your route to that promotion you've been hankering for.

'I'm on it, boss,' you say. 'You relax and enjoy your break.'

'You'll be fine. Just remember the law of unintended consequences. You never know what reactions your actions could cause.'

→ **Continue to page 154.**

Putin extends a finger and presses a button on his desk, and your chair starts descending into the floor. For a moment you think you're being dropped into a bear pit, and you wonder if you should have let someone know where you were going. But the chair descends smoothly through a shaft into a very different underground campus-like space full of funky beanbags, huddle spaces and colourfully attired twenty-somethings. It's the Moscow equivalent of Silicon Valley, right under the Kremlin.

'This is our campaign headquarters for the next election,' says Scarface, whose chair has descended along with yours.

'I thought the next Russian elections weren't for another four years?'

The FSB man looks momentarily confused. 'Oh, not for the Russian elections!' He chuckles and shakes his head, walking you past a bank of screens showing what looks like a league table of US swing states and Twitter handles.

The spy chief stops at a cluster of sofas where a young woman with spiky pink hair, dressed all in black, sits cross-legged typing at a laptop with stickers on it. You're getting a *Girl with the Dragon Tattoo* vibe – this is much more promising.

'This is Svetlana, our Fabergé of the meme,' the spy chief says. 'You've heard of Americans' legendary freedom? Svetlana is the one who decides what they do with it.'

She rolls her eyes and extends her hand for the briefcase.

'Don't worry. It won't affect her,' Scarface says. 'She has

the highest psychometrics for cynicism and jadedness we've ever seen. She's impervious.'

'It's one of the advantages of believing in nothing,' Svetlana adds.

'Now, if you'll excuse me, I'm heading off to my dacha. I don't wish to be in Moscow if fighting breaks out,' says Scarface.

Once he's resumed his chair and been elevated out of view, Svetlana looks at you. Then she looks at the briefcase. Then back at you.

'Well?'

→ **Give her the case. Turn to page 151.**

→ **Don't give her the case. You're not yet sure if you can trust her. Turn to page 135.**

A brief and undignified wrestling match later, you've managed to prise the key from Prof. Wu and let yourself out of the lab, leaving her yelling incoherently after you.

No way are you staying to save the bees after that performance. Now that you've seen how low she'll stoop – faking a bomb! – you're 100 per cent convinced that alarmist clock of hers is a trick, too, designed to entangle you. Ninety per cent convinced, anyway. There's no time to worry about it now, though. You're late for what's probably a very real apocalypse in Washington DC.

On the plane, you will the engines to spin faster. If Amber Lily has something civilisation-ending on his hands and you miss it, you'll have to explain why you wasted so much time on a non-apocalypse, and that'd be a true nightmare scenario.

→ **Continue to page 13.**

The sky above is clean and clear. All's well with the universe and you congratulate yourself smugly on making such strong choices.

The End

Uncanny Elon grins.

'Good morning,' it says. 'In case you're wondering how we Elon Musks spin so many high-tech plates – yes, there are six of us.'

It grins again. It's almost more unnerving than whatever's making all those sinkholes. Feeling a bit stupid talking to an android, you ask it what is going on under the ground.

'Let me explain what we do here in simple terms because you're a dummy,' the billionaire's plasticky twin says. The android seems to have been designed to be even truer to Musk's personality than to his appearance. 'We're making a tunnel-digging robot called the Really Freakishly Large Drill, but its AI engine worked a bit better than expected and it's developed an agenda of its own which isn't 100 per cent friendly to humanity. And another thing, we've lost all control of it. It can keep going by itself for a thousand years thanks to its onboard geothermal power station, so we can't switch it off, and it rewrites its own code constantly. It's completely walled itself off from our subroutines.'

Uncanny Elon shoots you a shit-eating smile that reminds you of your boss.

'We Elons are a teensy bit worried it's going to burrow under cities and basically tear a new one in the planet's mantle, leaving a string of volcanoes and earthquakes in its wake. Elon's taking care of it, though.'

Huh, this is an apocalypse scenario you've not heard of before. It could be good for your promotion chances to be known for dealing with something so rare. What's your first move?

→ **Ask him why they built something so dangerous. Turn to page 127.**

→ **Ask Uncanny Elon if it was him who called you. Turn to page 51.**

→ **Go and have a look at what Real Elon is doing on his holographic computer. Turn to page 97.**

→ **It's time to wage war on this giant gadget. To call your contact at the Pentagon turn to page 57.**

It was all going so well

A dark speck up where the birds soar is growing, and fast. Oof, you've been astronomically unlucky, and astronomically is the word because it's asteroid HJ12, seven cubic miles of rock travelling at 240,000mph, and it's about to send up a new doughnut-shaped mountain range the size of the Pyrenees, along with a dust cloud that will block out all light for the next year. The environment you've worked so hard to protect is going to be well and truly wrecked.

Does that mean you've wasted your life, that all that work has been meaningless?

Well, how can the meaning of a life's work depend on God throwing dice?

Such are the questions you mull as the dark shape in the sky slowly grows, casting the idyllic scene into shadow.

The End

The crying man looks up through reddened eyes and takes you in. 'You're who the UN sent, huh? I'm Chris Gordon. Fox News is calling me Gordon Sanitaire, you know, as in cordon sanitaire, because I'm the new chief epimediologist.'

'Do you mean epidemiologist?'

'That's what I said, isn't it? Anyway, you're far too late. We're all going to die horribly.'

'We're going to be fine; I deal with situations like this every day,' you say firmly, but privately you're worried. Dealing with a disease this awful requires a special person and you're not sure he's it. You flash him Svetlana's wholesome meme on your phone and he perks up, but a few seconds later he's snivelling into his collar once more.

Meanwhile, Trump has brought his televised address to a close and has begun yelling at the entire room.

'This is a problem that needs to be fixed – yesterday. I don't want any one of you coming back in here until you have solutions. I'm authorising you to do whatever it takes. Except no vaccines. Now scram.'

'Dad said scram!' adds Donald Trump Junior, who has joined his father behind the big desk.

'You too, Don,' says Trump and you can feel the awkwardness fill the room like a nasty gas. 'Ivanka, stay behind for a minute, honey.'

You shuffle out of the Oval Office with everyone else, noticing a lot of defeated-looking expressions under the protective gear.

'Tell me the situation,' you instruct the chief epidemiologist.

'Everyone just started coughing their asses up out of their ears and dying. I've had doctors telling me they don't know what to do, doctors dying. It's so bad, it's sooo gross.'

He takes you over to a window and you see lines of bodies left on stretchers on the White House lawn. One of the corpses' midriffs erupts like a volcano of cold chicken soup as you watch. The chief epidemiologist makes a noise like he is about to be sick.

'We're going to fix this,' you say with a certainty you don't feel. 'But first I need a hazmat suit.'

What's your first move?

→ **Ask him where the disease came from. Turn to page 54.**

→ **Ask him if they've made any progress on developing a vaccine. Turn to page 130.**

→ **Tell him to seal off the city immediately. Turn to page 60.**

Choosing to ignore the android version, you ask the real Elon Musk how he plans to stop his Really Freakishly Large Drill, but he declines to answer.

'What's your problem with us anyway?' you say. 'We're just trying to save the world, you know.'

He continues ignoring you, so you stand right where his holographic screen is until he finally looks up angrily.

'My problem with your organisation? You're encouraging the illusion we can save ourselves. One of these days *something* will get us. It's simple entropy. That's why we need to become a multi-planetary civilisation ASAP. Now, please get out of my holo-space.'

'Are you like this with plumbers?' you ask him, as a very strong pair of non-human hands lift you clean off the ground and set you down to one side, allowing Elon to continue completely ignoring you.

→ **If you want to understand what's going on it looks like you're going to have to speak to Uncanny Elon after all. Turn to page 118.**

Your boss's advice makes sense – you'll head to DC and cross your fingers that a lid can be kept on whatever's happening in China. After working three nights in a row, though, you're so very tired . . . Sitting in the departure lounge at Sheremetyevo Airport, your eyelids feel like they have breeze blocks tied to them. You decide to nap now while you have the chance.

You wake with a start, still in the departure lounge. Dawn light is streaming in, all the shops are shut, and your plane must be long gone. How long were you asleep?

Damn it, your phone alarm didn't go off.

The feel-good effect of the countermeme has abandoned you now, leaving an unpleasant groggy sensation that's compounded by the memory of an unnerving dream you were having. You'd been assigned to stop dinosaurs devouring fleeing crowds on the steps of the Capitol. Then it turned nightmarish when you realised you weren't wearing any trousers.

You're going to have to find a new flight in a hurry.

→ **Continue to page 13.**

You wander over to a tank with a wonky honeycomb inside and scoop out a glob of the good stuff with your index finger. Prof. Wu seems unimpressed – and, on tasting the honey, so are you. It tastes like sauerkraut.

These are some seriously confused insect chefs.

Just then a video call comes in. It must be President Xi himself.

→ **Answer the call. Turn to page 44.**

'Why did you build this thing anyway?' you ask Uncanny Elon, who happily launches into a sales pitch.

'The Really Freakishly Large Drill is the culmination of Musk technologies. Based around the operating system developed for the Tesla Model X, it features an infinitely scalable neural net from OpenAI, ten-metre cobalt drill bit from the Boring Company, and the same engine as the Falcon Heavy rocket, all for the price of a family saloon car. So when Earth becomes uninhabitable, you too can terraform a new cave dwelling on the planet of your choice. Now with free shoulder-mounted bazooka for every round-one investor.'

'Er, count me out,' you tell it.

→ **Turn back to page 118.**

The turkey looks up at you gratefully with those bottomless black eyes, and for once you feel you've done something right. But what next?

→ **Turn to page 78 to try another course of action.**

You ask your client for a look at the meme.

She shakes her head firmly. 'It's too dangerous.'

You protest – if you can keep your sanity in the face of a giant super-intelligent robot worm twerking in front of you, surely it's safe for you to view an especially persuasive jpeg? – but she is not having it.

'The Secretary General insisted on seeing it too. He couldn't understand why we were making so much fuss about a picture. Fifteen minutes later he was screaming at a pot plant. Said it was an enemy of the people and a single-issue crybaby.'

You notice she's gone a bit green around the gills.

'Would you excuse me, I think the oysters from earlier might have been bad?'

And she hurries off to the ladies', leaving the attaché case on the table between you. In the privacy of the dining booth, this is your chance to peek inside the case.

→ **Open the case. Turn to page 74.**

→ **Don't risk it. Wait for her to return. Turn to page 90.**

'Tell me I misheard and Trump hasn't really ruled out developing a vaccine?' you ask the chief epidemiologist.

He glances fleetingly to his right, where Donald Trump Junior is idly polishing a pair of scissors.

'No way, vaccines would just make us sicker,' the chief epidemiologist says loudly, and then when Donald Junior has moved off down the corridor, continues in a low voice: 'The last person in my job got canned for trying to make a vaccine, so keep it quiet, OK? This is an anti-vaxx zone, at least as far as the family are concerned.'

You nod. 'Show me what you've got.'

The chief epidemiologist shrugs. 'Our organs will all have evacuated our bodies long before a vaccine's even close to ready. But sure, if you want.'

He waits until the coast is clear before leaning on the wall, causing a section of West Wing panelling to yield and reveal a steel lift shaft in which you're soon travelling down to floor -10.

'There's an elevator a bit like this in the Kremlin,' you say conversationally.

'Maybe a few people could survive down here in the biolab,' he says. 'Come out in a few years to repopulate. Not me, though, I don't have the stomach for it.'

The lift opens on a stark white airlock thingy that blasts you with a disinfecting white mist. 'This place was going to be a golf course for George W. Bush, but they made it into a biolab instead after the anthrax attacks in 2001.'

As the second airlock door is opening, a crocodile of white lab rats runs down the side wall past you into the lift behind. You exchange worried looks with the chief epidemiologist. Ahead, in the biolab, a pair of white boots sticks out from beneath a lab bench. You hurry in, but you're very definitely too late to save this unfortunate scientist. It looks like a microwave lasagne has exploded under his visor.

A quick search of the room reveals two more personnel in the same condition.

'Even this place is contaminated,' you murmur.

Examining one of the bodies, you find a horizontal tear across the lower back part of the hazmat suit, concealed under the air supply unit. You flip one of the other bodies and find the exact same tear in the same place, just where it might slip a cursory check of the suit.

'This was sabotage,' you announce gravely.

'I told you finding a vaccine was a waste of time. Do you fancy finding somewhere peaceful to sit and eat pain-killers?'

He's under a lot of stress, you get that, but the chief epidemiologist's attitude is making it very difficult for you to stay positive. One thing is more contagious than Virus X, you think to yourself – and that's negativity.

→ **Search the biolab. Turn to page 37.**

→ **Go back and try something else. Turn to page 78.**

You're not sure what you expected meme-smithing to involve, but Svetlana's approach seems to involve hanging upside down by her legs for long periods of time, sighing, and only very occasionally touching her laptop. You feel you should give her space to work, but there's a screen showing a livestream of the RT news channel in the corner, and the mute footage shows that the chaos in Europe is only worsening and spreading by the minute.

'Everything going all right?' you ask politely as you bring her third energy drink of the evening.

'Terrible. This is the best I've got.'

She swivels her screen to show a stock image of a multi-ethnic high five with the legend LIFE'S ALWAYS BETTER WHEN WE WORK TOGETHER. Before you can give a diplomatic verdict, Svetlana slaps the laptop shut and dives headfirst into a pile of beanbags. Muffled swearing follows.

'My whole career has been about polarising people, turning differences into divides. Now I'm supposed to be a healer? I have no feeling for this work!'

You're starting to get it; she really is an artist of the meme.

'Is there a joyful feeling you could bring to mind to inspire you? A favourite song perhaps? Or maybe a memory from your childhood.'

She shakes her head contemptuously, but you refuse to believe she can't summon a glimmer of feeling for her fellow humans.

You'll need to help Svetlana find faith in people again, or she'll never craft a unifying meme.

→ **Ask Svetlana to tell you her life story. You need to get at the root cause of her cynicism. Turn to page 23.**

→ **Restore her faith in humanity by reading her wholesome stories from the internet. Turn to page 88.**

You make your way over to the chichi furniture store with the loud music. Initially your eyes can't make sense of the snake tangle of writhing, pumping, grunting bodies on the nice sectional leather sofa in the window. There are approximately eight participants in the orgy. Going on nine: the chief epidemiologist has begun the cumbersome task of removing the pieces of his hazmat suit.

'This is where I stop,' he says.

'That's not a great idea in terms of infection control,' you say, having to repeat yourself over the house version of 'Auld Lang Syne' coming out of the store speakers.

'I'm bowing out here,' the chief epidemiologist says. 'I want to die in the throes of carnal oblivion.'

You could try to stop him. But the man's an adult, and besides, one thing is becoming obvious: you're not going to be saving anyone today.

As you contemplate returning to Trump to tell him everyone is doomed, you hear a crash behind you and turn to see a Harley Davidson skidding along the road on its side. The rider has spilled off and is heaving and vomiting on the asphalt, obviously infected.

You look back at the bike. The key is still in the ignition.

→ **Go back to Trump and tell him the world is doomed. Turn to page 146.**

→ **You can't bear to face your failure. Ride away from all this. Turn to page 144.**

'I'm not sure I'm ready to give you this,' you tell Svetlana, tightening your grip on the briefcase. She grabs your wrist, turns you, and, before you know what's happened, she's in possession of the case and you're on your back like a turtle.

'OK, I'm ready to trust you now,' you wheeze. You've seen movies, and as a rule of thumb, the punk hacker grrrl who knows krav maga is the one whose side you want to be on.

→ **Continue to page 151.**

Kim Jong-un roars with laughter, banging the table with his fist, narrowly avoiding instigating oblivion

Kim Jong-un's voice is deep and commanding. 'May my father's spirit and the cheering of the people bring our glorious rocket smashing down on the American lair! Let us sever the windpipe of the Great Rapscallion and prove our glorious prestige for a thousand years! And if the western devils send rockets back at us, I personally will knock them out of the sky with my peerless golfing skill.'

The generals cower in silence.

Then Kim Jong-un begins to roar with laughter. 'I'm joking, you guys! That's the old me. I want to clear up this mess as much as you do!'

Tears of laughter roll down his round cheeks. One by one the military officials start laughing too, and a desperate mirth fills the room.

→ **Join in the laughter. Turn to page 61.**

→ **Keep a reproachful silence; this is no time for messing around. Turn to page 75.**

If anyone can help you rid the realm of this dangerous meme it's the man behind the social media curtain, Facebook boss Mark Zuckerberg. But first you have to figure out how to get in touch with him. Thinking his number may be on file, you ring the office; Christmas is over so someone might be around to have a dig for you.

Excusing yourself, you stand out in the corridor and place a call back to base. It rings through to answerphone.

'This is the Department for Continuity (Global). We can't take your call right now but did you know you can now register cataclysmic events on our website? Go to—'

You ring off. You try your boss, but he's on answerphone too. The only other person you can think of who might have some kind of connection to Zuckerberg is your colleague Susan, whom you could call in Chamonix, though you're loath to let her steal your glory.

→ **Call Susan anyway. Turn to page 72.**

→ **No way, you're not giving her the satisfaction. Try to create a countermeme instead. Turn to page 82.**

Just fifteen minutes later, you're rising up from the White House lawn in an Apache military helicopter. Donald Trump Junior stands below, waving you off, a puckered little smile visible through his hazmat mask before the helicopter gains altitude and shifts off over the Potomac.

'Weird kid,' comments the chief epidemiologist.

The streets in the centre of the city appear quiet, but as the chopper continues east, you see lines of abandoned vehicles blocking the roads. Thousands of people displaced by the outbreak are pressed up against coils of barbed wire that cut across the I-20. On the far side, a few tanks and a sparse line of troops appear woefully inadequate to the task of keeping the blockade intact. Even as you watch, the crowd surges toward the wire and one of the soldiers has to fire a warning burst of machine-gun fire into the sky.

From your aerial viewpoint you see what the soldiers cannot: a group of lobbyists with wirecutters are sneaking up on an unguarded section of barbed wire away from the highway. One of them coughs into his necktie.

'Down there!' you cry out.

→ **They're infected! You've got to land the chopper and stop them getting away. Turn to page 24.**

→ **It's pointless trying to quarantine an entire city. Head back to the White House and try something else. Turn back to page 73.**

You cough and periodically say, 'Excuse me, Mr Musk, sir', until Musk finally flips and says, 'My super-intelligent autonomous subterranean tunnel-boring robot, the Really Freakishly Large Drill, has malfunctioned and there's a 62 per cent chance it will undermine the structure of the earth's mantle.'

You only understand about one word in three of this, and he must be able to see your incomprehension as he says, 'My drilling robot has gone mad. It can go through granite like butter. And it's totally unstoppable. Are those words short enough for you? But I've got it under control, more or less.'

Elon Musk returns to his holographic labours, while the android version grins at you awkwardly. From what you can understand, you've got to stop this drill from somehow turning the whole planet inside out, but where to start?

→ **Talk to Uncanny Elon. Maybe he'll have more answers. Turn to page 118.**

→ **Ask the real Elon what he's doing to stop the drill. Turn to page 124.**

With the pilot and chief epidemiologist by your side, you begin the journey back to the White House. Though it's only a few miles, in your hazmat suits no walk is easy. Shadows lengthen over the eerily quiet streets; most of those left alive in the city are staying indoors. Here and there you see the bodies of people ravaged by the disease, struck down so fast they expired in the street.

'The whole world will be like this pretty soon, I guess,' the chief epidemiologist says, cheerful as usual. 'Deader than a desert. Look at that, someone's looted Max Mara.'

You and the pilot manage an eyeroll through the plastic of your suits but you have a feeling the chief epidemiologist's gloomy outlook is aligned with reality right now. An enemy that kills and spreads at this speed cannot be stopped, and for the first time you realise the true gravity of the situation. To have let Pink Camellia bring about a thermonuclear war at the start of the week would have been one thing, but you're now on track for the most apocalypses stopped in one week since the legendary UNC(G) consultant Verolina Lang's historic six-apocalypse streak during the Cold War. Defeat at this stage would be as galling as choosing the wrong box right at the end of *Deal or No Deal*.

As you reach K Street you hear thumping dance music coming from a designer furniture store.

→ **Go over to investigate. Turn to page 134.**

→ **Head back to the White House and try something else. There's no time to lose. Turn to page 78.**

Your minder is fuming outside the Ops room, but you manage to duck his grasp and go inside. Kim Jong-un and the generals are right where you left them.

'Kim Jong-un,' you begin, 'I need you to remember the missile's deactivation code. The world needs you to remember it.'

The generals stiffen but Kim Jong-un waves your impertinent question away.

'Not this again. I do not know any deactivation code, fix-it person! Therefore there never was one, as I have perfect recall. Isn't that so, comrades?'

The generals all nod. 'Not only that, you are perfect in every way, Supreme Leader.'

You decide to appeal to the generals. 'So not one of you remembers the Chairman here setting a deactivation code back in 2016 or 2017? Remember, your very survival depends on it.'

There is a long pause. Finally an ancient general rises to his feet. 'Chairman of the People, I recall you *did* choose a deactivation code that no one else was allowed to know.'

Sweat beads on the old man's brow and he sits back down. You get the feeling he just used up all his courage in one go.

You've so far been oddly impressed by Kim Jong-un's levity on the brink, but now he has a sense of humour failure. 'So I forgot something, is that it? Well, maybe it's true! Maybe I did!' He glares from face to face, as if challenging the room, but you're also not sure if he might be about to cry. 'And maybe I have to eat and defecate as well, and maybe my dad and my grandpa did as well! Is that what you want to hear? That we had to put our trousers on one leg at a time and we're disgusting human beings just like the rest of you?'

The generals all look at their hands.

When Kim Jong-un speaks again he sounds suddenly tired. 'Ah well, maybe I did forget the code. It was three years ago. Do you remember your passwords from back then?' Then he lights up. 'Wait a second, I think I just remembered it!'

Kim Jong-un brings up a dialogue box on the creaky old computer and carefully types in a series of letters while everyone watches tensely.

The computer makes a discouraging beep.

Incorrect code entered. One attempt remaining.

'Oh,' says the Chairman, and you can tell this isn't one of his funny jokes.

→ **The correct code simply must be in his memory somewhere. Try using hypnosis to recover it. Turn to page 36.**

→ **This is hopeless. But there's still time to warn the Americans and save thousands of lives if they can evacuate New York before impact. Turn to page 18.**

'Hey, where are you going?' the chopper pilot calls, as you straddle the Harley. No time for goodbyes. You flare the throttle and speed off.

Soon you've fled the city through the same gap in the barbed wire that earlier today you were trying to guard, and you're away down the freeway, heading west. You have a long journey ahead of you and no time to lose.

→ **Continue to page 20.**

'What's wrong with you?' Kim Jong-un asks. 'Don't you have a funny bone?'

Failing to make you smile, he pulls some funny faces and barks like a seal. The generals all take their cue to fall about with practised laughter.

'When is the rocket due to re-enter the atmosphere?' you interject, trying to bring them back on track.

Kim Jong-un stares at you intimidatingly. 'You don't think I'm a funny guy?'

Uh oh, it looks like you're in a reverse *Goodfellas* situation – but you're determined to hold your nerve.

'Take him to the cells!' Kim Jong-un orders. A fat guard grabs you around the middle and starts hauling you out of the room. You think one of your ribs may be about to crack when Kim Jong-un explodes into giggles. 'I'm kidding! Deng, put the foreigner down! What must you think of me?'

Deng sheepishly lets you go as the generals once again provide the laugh track.

You've had it. You pick up a jug of water and slosh it over the Dear Leader's iconic visage. The room instantly hushes as if you've doused them all and Kim Jong-un's mouth opens and shuts in shock before he bursts into his strongest gale of hysterics yet.

'Very good!' he guffaws. 'Very good! You're a joker like me.'

→ **Continue to page 61.**

When you are finally shown into the Oval Office, Trump is watching a DVD of his election night coverage, while his surviving staff mill around with panic-stricken faces. When he sees you he puts down his popcorn and booms, 'It's the UN patsy! What have you got for us, patsy?'

This isn't easy for you to admit. You've stopped nuclear missiles and crazed AIs and killer memes but this time you've got nothing.

'There's simply nothing we can do,' you say.

'The World Police need my help, huh? Only I can fix it?'

'No, Mr President. I'm saying there's literally nothing anyone can do.'

'Then you're fired.'

Someone has a word in Trump's ear. A grave mood settles over the room.

'There is *one* thing we can do.'

The officials turn in unison as Donald Junior steps boldly into the centre of the room.

'I'm only going to suggest this because it's so clear the situation is hopeless. Why is it that we have all been able to survive and function in this tainted environment? It's because we're strong, not like the dead, right, Dad? But it's also because of these. Our hazmat suits. We love our hazmat suits, don't we, Pop?'

He ventures a look at the President.

'A hazmat suit is your own personal wall, if you like. It stops alien organisms from getting into our healthy American bodies. So here's my pitch: why can't all Americans have one?'

The aides all murmur.

'Over 700 million people walking around in hazmat suits?' someone says. 'You can't be serious.'

'And the global market is even bigger. The virus is guaranteed to spread, turning seven billion people into potential customers who'd be prepared to pay thousands of dollars to protect their health and loved ones.'

You gawp. 'But that would take years to organise even under ideal conditions. Now? Logistically impossible.'

'Fortunately, Dad has one long-term thinker on his team. I've taken care of it,' Donald Junior says with the jubilant air of one who is closing a sale. 'Trucks, trains and ships full of Trump Freedom Suits™ are even now arriving in major urban centres around the planet, ready to sell.'

Trump lumbers to his feet and envelops Donald Junior in a hug. 'My son.'

Some of the longer-serving members of staff break into applause, and you sense this is the denouement of a long-running family soap opera.

Whether you like it or not, a course of action has been chosen.

→ **Continue to page 58.**

You repeat your idea to your client. The meme is already out there; it stands to reason the only way to reverse the slide into chaos is to create a countermeme.

'A countermeme? Is that possible?' your client says, brightening. 'Torsten, come over here. Torsten is our whizzkid.'

A portly gentleman in his fifties wanders across the floor with a glass of sherry. You're no technical expert but this guy doesn't inspire confidence. What kind of hacker wears a cravat?

'A countermeme? Interesting,' Torsten says cautiously. 'We could certainly put together a working group, commission a report or two?'

'We don't have time for this,' you say. 'We need to make a countermeme *now* or they'll tear us to shreds!'

Torsten shakes his head ponderously and plucks a canapé from a passing tray with lizardlike skill. 'Creating a countermeme is harder than you perhaps imagine. Selecting an image that doesn't breach Article 14 for copyright infringement, writing a funny caption that all twenty-seven nations can agree to . . . it would require experience, resources and, frankly, a level of sheer cunning that I'm proud to say we do not have in Europe.'

And maybe he's right. But he's given you an idea. The EU may not have the requisite meme-making experience, but you know who might.

→ **Continue to page 79.**

'The clock thing nearly convinced me,' you tell Prof. Wu. 'But I don't buy it. Anything could happen in four years – we'll probably have invented robot bees by then. So I'm sorry, but I'm going to Washington DC. You'll be receiving an invoice for my travel expenses.'

'I thought you might say that as well.' She sighs. 'So I made some preparations.' And with that she hits a button on the wall, causing a security door to rattle down from the ceiling and block your exit. 'Did you really think I'd let you leave so easily after a year of ignoring my messages?'

You watch open-mouthed as she removes the casing from the Clock of No Return to show you packed brown cylinders and wires inside.

'W-what is that?'

'Oh, that's just eighty kilogrammes of C-4 explosive, enough to blow this place up and kill us both.'

'You'd kill yourself?'

'A bee would, to save the hive.'

Uh oh, she's deadly serious. What do you want to do now?

→ **Try to force the door and make your escape. Turn to page 89.**

→ **Reason with her. As a senior scientist she must have been an intelligent person once. Turn to page 5.**

You place a quick call to your new friend Kim Jong-un and quickly explain the situation.

'Sure, I can have a word with my friend Xi Jinping,' Kim Jong-un says. 'What number shall I have him call?'

You give Prof. Wu a thumbs-up. Life's easy when you're in the club. Now you just have to wait for Xi himself to call you back.

What do you want to do while you wait?

→ **Those bumblebees look sleepy. Knock on their tank to wake them up. Turn to page 109.**

→ **Sample the local honey. Turn to page 126.**

Svetlana holds the case carefully, lowers her nose to it and inhales deeply as if it were a good Malbec.

You hold your breath as she opens the laptop to view the meme. You get ready to try to wrestle her to the ground if she flips out, but her only reaction is to raise an eyebrow.

'It's not one of ours, but it's very fine work, very fine,' Svetlana murmurs. 'Who created this?'

You tell her you don't know.

'Do the initials SB mean anything to you? If you zoom right into the bottom left-hand corner it's written into the pixels. He or she couldn't resist signing their work.'

Someone with the initials SB who operates in the shadows and wants to see the break-up of Europe? You make a mental note to make some enquiries.

'So anyway, you want me to create a countermeme, right? Hmm. What's my motivation exactly?'

'This meme is on its way to destroying everything that's good in this world.'

'Why would I stand in its way? If I were you, trying to persuade me to help you, I would say that I should be the only one creating anything this evil. Plus, if this thing spreads unchecked there'll be nothing left for me to undermine, which doesn't sound fun.'

'OK, what you just said,' you reply feebly, feeling like you're being eaten for breakfast.

'Fine. I'll help!'

→ **Stay with Svetlana and see if you can help her work. Turn to page 132.**

In the lift to the UN Department for Continuity (Global), you put your doubts about the way the Virus X outbreak was resolved to one side. Maybe that's just how things are now, a series of apocalypses and adaptations, headlines that come and go unnoticed and unremarked.

You think instead of the reception that awaits you. Virus X aside, you've just helped the world through a series of cataclysms in almost unprecedented quick succession. You're bound to get a promotion and a salary boost, maybe even a meeting room named after you. Your boss has probably organised a party to honour your achievements and announce you as his newest senior continuity consultant. There may be cake.

You come out of your reverie when you notice that the Freedom-Suited figure who's just squeezed into the lift is none other than your boss. You greet him and he peers through your visor to see who you are.

'How was your Christmas break?' he says offhandedly.

And all your daydreams crash into pieces. He apparently doesn't even remember putting you on duty.

'By the way, a Level Five came in from the CERN laboratory in Geneva this morning,' your boss says as you come out of the lift. 'Looks like they've bashed together a couple of particles they shouldn't have and got a mini black hole on their hands. It's already eaten two technicians and an artist in residence. That's a situation that's going to need skill and experience so I'm sending Susan. You can work on updating the Fate-a-Base here, OK?'